Book Marketing Made Easy

Simple Strategies for Selling Your Nonfiction Book Online

by D'vorah Lansky

*"The author always has the greatest amount of
passion and enthusiasm for his or her particular book.
As an author, you have to take that passion and use it to
propel you forward to look for opportunities to
tell people about your book."*

Terry Whalin, Publisher
Intermedia Publishing Group

June 2011
ISBN 978-0-9651975-9-5

Published by:

Desktop Wings Inc.
700 East Walnut Street
Perkasie, PA 18944
215-453-9312
www.desktopwings.com

Book Marketing Made Easy

Simple Strategies for
Selling Your
Nonfiction Book
Online

Dedication

To Auntie Gail,

Thank you for all your love and support
and for spurring me on to such a
high standard of excellence!

In Praise of
Book Marketing Made Easy

"The pages of *Book Marketing Made Easy* are packed with practical ideas. Read carefully, and then repeatedly take action to apply the skills to your book. D'vorah Lansky is a skilled teacher who knows these strategies because she practices them."

> **W. Terry Whalin**, author of *Jumpstart Your Publishing Dreams*
> www.TerryWhalin.com

"If you think online book marketing is nothing more than Facebook, Twitter, and LinkedIn, D'vorah Lansky will blow your mind. Add to that a really cool section on repurposing existing material into new revenue streams, a ton of specific resources, and a clear, accessible style, and you get a must-read for any author who'd like to actually be successful."

> **Shel Horowitz**, author of *Grassroots Marketing for Authors and Publishers*
> www.GrassrootsMarketingforAuthors.com

"New and established authors will find a wealth of practical advice for online book promotion in this well-organized book. The in-depth chapter on teleseminars is a real gem."

> **Dana Lynn Smith**, author of *The Savvy Book Marketer Guides*
> www.SavvyBookMarketer.com

"D'vorah Lansky gets it. She understands the importance of perpetual promotion to make a book successful. *Book Marketing Made Easy* overflows with valuable and do-able information. It contains inside scoop that I have not found anywhere else. A 'must-have' for the serious publisher."

> **Brian Jud**, author of *How to Make Real Money Selling Books*, and *Beyond the Bookstore*
> www.BookMarketingWorks.com

"Marketing is an essential skill for every author who dreams of making a living with their writing. The challenge is not knowing where to begin. Enter *Book Marketing Made Easy*. Covering numerous highly applicable online marketing strategies, *Book Marketing Made Easy* will benefit any author who wants to sell lots of books, gain visibility, and be viewed as the 'go to' expert."

"In addition to marketing know-how, readers will learn proven systems to create multiple streams of revenue in simple to apply ways. D'vorah Lansky's *Book Marketing Made Easy* is a must have for any author serious about being an author."

> **Kathleen Gage**, Book Marketing Expert and Internet Marketing Advisor
> www.KathleenGage.com

"Dvorah Lansky has put it all together in her new book, *Book Marketing Made Easy*. She gave me, a book coach who teaches these strategies, some great "ah-has" such as her inspiring interview techniques in her chapter on teleseminar promotion. Talk about easy! My book sales went way up after I experienced these techniques first-hand, when D'vorah interviewed me as part of her teleseminar series! This book can help you monetize your teleseminars too."

> **Judy Cullins**, author of *LinkedIn Marketing: 8 Best Tactics to Build Book and Business Sales*
> www.BookCoaching.com

"Brilliant! *Book Marketing Made Easy* is a perfect take-you-by-the-hand how-to guide for selling more books faster. Get it, read it, and use it; you *will* sell more books while simultaneously increasing your fame."

> **Daniel Hall**, Author, Speaker, and Marketer Extraordinaire
> www.RealFastBook.com

"In *Book Marketing Made Easy*, D'vorah Lansky provides readers with a wealth of practical, easy-to-use tips and guidance. This down-to-earth manual is an essential tool for any author approaching online nonfiction book promotion."

> **Beth Kallman Werner**, Founder and President, Author Connections, LLC
> www.AuthorConnections.com

Foreword

Books are the quietest and most constant of friends; they are the most accessible and wisest of counselors, and the most patient of teachers.

Charles W. Eliot, Author, 1834-1926

Authors write books to fulfill many dreams: dreams of sharing their wisdom, dreams of transforming the world, dreams of becoming famous, and dreams of inspiring their readers. It is easy for an aspiring author to fantasize about appearing on a famous talk show, selling millions of copies of her book, riding in black limousines to meet with movie producers, and spending happy hours autographing books for adoring readers.

These dreams and visions give authors the fortitude to write books. Writing isn't easy. It requires long hours of hard work, facing your fears of judgment and rejection, and the humbling experience of having an editor point out all your grammatical errors. If authors did not have those dreams and visions of success to propel them forward, they would quit and the world would be lessened from the loss of their book.

As a publisher and book consultant, I see authors struggle with one area above all others: book marketing. Many tell me that they would rather write another book than market the book they just completed.

This is understandable. Book marketing can be overwhelming, especially to first time authors.

In *Book Marketing Made Easy*, D'vorah Lansky provides an invaluable service for authors by explaining how to use the Internet to market your book. She does this by providing clear, step-by-step instructions that remove overwhelm and confusion, replacing them with knowledge and confidence. She teaches you how to market your book online. When you finish reading this book, you will believe that you can market your book, and that belief is the cornerstone of successful book marketing.

When you follow the advice in this practical and clear guide, you will be able to take concrete action to market your book online without spending a fortune on hiring others to promote your book for you. While you may decide to expand your book marketing efforts in the future, every author can benefit from following these simple steps to build an Internet presence for your book.

Let me encourage you to read this book with an open mind and a curious nature. Explore all the different options offered to you, and start working with the ideas that appeal to you the most. Plan to build your marketing over time, just as you wrote your book one page at a time. By taking daily marketing action, as D'vorah so wisely advises, you'll be able to build momentum and create sustainable sales for your book.

Your book is valuable. It provides wisdom, information, and knowledge that is unique because it is filtered through your life experiences. There are readers who are waiting for your book to solve their problems and enhance their lives.

Please take the actions required to get that wonderful book of yours into the hands of those readers. When you follow the steps in this book, you will be well on the way to transforming the world with the wisdom in your book.

To Your Book Marketing Success,

Lynne Klippel
Best-Selling Author, Publisher, and Book Consultant
www.BusinessBuildingBooks.com

Table of Contents

Introduction

Congratulations, it is an incredible accomplishment to write and publish a book. Marketing your book is just the next step in the process. In *Book Marketing Made Easy*, we will examine the key facets of online book marketing as a way to bring you more exposure, more book sales and more clients.

You may ask, "Whose primary responsibility is marketing, and why?" Many of us assume that our publisher is going to market our book, but publishers release many books each season and need to be selective as to where they allocate their time and resources. When it comes down to it, no one has as much interest in seeing a book succeed as the author. Unless you are a best-selling author, or your publisher sees the potential for you to become one, you are on your own when it comes to marketing your book, for the most part.

The reason why so many authors do so many readings, book signings, and interviews is that they realize the importance of getting in front of their audience, to share the message of their book. It is a form of *propulsion*, either self-imposed or at the request of their publisher or agent. These authors are physically spreading their passion and enthusiasm into the marketplace.

In this book, we will focus on powerful yet simple, *online* book marketing strategies. You will discover the secrets that successful authors use to market their books online. In *Book Marketing Made Easy* you will learn how to:

- Increase your credibility and be seen as an expert in your field.

- Sell more books to people who will benefit from your message.

- Create multiple sources of income with the content of your book.

- Harness the power of multi-media marketing to reach more people.

- Use social media to increase your influence and expand your market.

As you prepare to market your book, spend some time remembering why it is you wrote it. Focus on your future readers and how your message can help them. As human beings, the desire to serve and help others often outweighs the drive for personal gain. Certainly, we want to generate an income from all of our intense labor, but when the focus shifts away from "how can I make more money or sell more books" to "how can I help more people with my message," we are able to get out of our own way. Our marketing becomes more about serving others and thus it is easier to promote our work.

Your book is a gift that you give to the world. There are people who are hungry for your message and you can help them, and impact their lives in positive ways, by sharing it. Your book is a legacy that you leave for yourself, your family, and the human race. Your book can make a difference for people. Approach the marketing of your book with this understanding and you will touch more lives and make more money while making a difference in this world.

If you can say what your book will do for someone and then, in a sentence or two, explain how it will benefit him, you not only have the fuel to *propel* your marketing engine, you have a powerful statement that you can share when people ask what your book is about.

Spend some time reflecting on why you wrote your book, what problem it solves for people and how they will benefit by reading it. For example, if you are writing a book on sales techniques for real estate agents, your problem-benefit statement might be something like, "My book teaches real estate professionals how to build lasting relationships with their prospects and clients, and make more sales." That's certainly clear.

The first step of book marketing is to figure out how your book specifically helps your readers. Then, every time you reach a stumbling block, you will be able to stop thinking about yourself and continue thinking about your readers. Picture them getting that benefit from your book and it will *propel* you forward.

John Kremer, author of *1001 Ways to Market Your Books,* says "Do something every day to market each of your books—for three years." This is powerful advice because little steps with consistent effort—done over time—will yield amazing results. This statement also brings to light the importance of continuing to market each of your books, even when you go on to publish your next book.

In *Book Marketing Made Easy,* you will have access to a wide variety of online book marketing strategies. I recommend that you read this book with a highlighter or notecards in hand. Highlight or jot down the marketing tips and ideas that speak to you. At the beginning of the week, select three to five of those cards or highlighted sections and complete those marketing activities. Repeat this practice weekly and you will be building a solid marketing campaign. Marketing your book is not something you do just when the book is newly published; marketing is an ongoing activity.

You may want to schedule book marketing time into your calendar. For example you may say, "Every afternoon from 2:00 to 3:00, I am going to work on book marketing." To take things a step further, you can jot down what specific book marketing activity you will be focused on during that time. This is where your highlighted points and notecards come in handy.

If you do something for your book every day, then by the end of the week you should feel proud of yourself and give yourself a reward. Do whatever makes you happy: spend time reading your favorite novel, go for a walk, take a bubble bath, or go out to the movies with friends or family. Take pride in your accomplishments and reward yourself with something special.

Developing Your Author Platform

An author platform is a place where people can come to connect with you. It is where you share your message and it refers to the size of your following/readership and your presence on the Internet. The number one thing that a publicist, publisher, agent, speaker's bureau, and people in the media want to know is: *who are you and why will people listen to you?* They want to see that you have a presence, especially on the Internet. It is essential for an author to have an author platform. Your platform raises your visibility and allows people to get acquainted with you.

People in the media want to know what you sound like and what you look like before having you on their show. Thus, producing audio and video recordings will strengthen your author platform. Here are a few things that you can do:

- Set your website up so that it makes a positive statement about you as an author. If you have any intentions of speaking, you are going to need a website which actually shows people who you are and what you speak about.

- Have a media page or speaker sheet that can be easily accessed on your website. Include low-resolution and high-resolution images of both you and your book cover.

- Outline a talk that you give related to your book. You can include five bullet points, or a list of sample questions, that you can cover.

- Include a brief and an expanded bio and your contact information. When composing your bio, rather than beginning by listing your credentials, begin by speaking about your strengths as a speaker or captivating presenter. For example, you might say, "D'vorah is a dynamic and engaging presenter." It is important that your bio talks about you as a speaker, in addition to listing your credentials.

- Add a page to your website that lists your speeches, events, presentations and programs.

- Include a section, on your media page, that links to your videos and recorded interviews.

- Make sure that you have a professional presence on the social media networks. Social networks provide you with the ability to reach a large number of people easily, develop your presence, share your expertise and impart the message of your book.

In this book, I will be sharing seven essential online marketing strategies: relationship marketing, blogging, social networking, promoting your book with teleseminars, information marketing, article marketing, and video marketing.

Each of these strategies has its foundation in relationship marketing, where you will learn the importance of building relationships first and marketing second. When it comes down to it, "people don't care how much you know, until they know how much you care!"

Chapter One:
Essentials of
Online Relationship Marketing

The foundation of this book is built on online relationship marketing strategies and techniques. From developing an online hub with your blog, to sending greeting cards to people who purchase your books or enroll in your book related programs, to producing videos as a way for people to see and hear you, to developing a strong social media presence, relationship marketing can be your secret to success by setting you apart from your competition and helping you to create a strong community of raving fans. By building a relationship with your audience, you will sell more books and become known as an expert in your field.

What is Relationship Marketing?

Relationship marketing deals with selling *second* and building relationships *first*. Where old-school marketing focuses on clever or salesy ways of convincing people to buy what you are selling, relationship marketing focuses on creating a connection with your audience so that they come to know, like, and trust you.

As an author, building relationships with your audience will not only allow you to sell more books, but will increase your following.

I was walking through a book store recently and overheard a conversation. Someone said, "I don't care how professional he is. If I don't like the guy I'm not going to do business with him." That is the essence of relationship marketing, having people become raving fans of yours and having them refer you to other people without your even asking.

The reason you want to know about relationship marketing is because that is the way you are going to grow your business: by building relationships with people. They are going to want to know you and they are going to want to buy your books and participate in your programs.

Weave Relationship Marketing Through Your Online Marketing Campaign

There are many ways to strengthen the connection between you and your audience. Find ways to be of service and to add value to your message. Share your knowledge and expertise via free content as well as through programs that people pay for; you will be helping people who can benefit from your message. Provide your audience with a variety of ways to connect with you and be authentic and caring. Demonstrate that you care about people first and making money second, and your business will grow.

Develop a Competitive Edge by Building Relationships with Your Email Subscribers

Your most important online asset is your list of email subscribers. These are people who opt-in to receive something from you in exchange for their name and email address. One of the most important things you can do to achieve success online is to build a solid relationship with your email subscribers. This can make the difference between a one-time sale and making a customer for life.

Here are a few ways to strengthen rapport with email subscribers:

- **Keep in touch often with people who have subscribed to your email list.** Do not email them only when you want to promote a product. Share tips, ideas, and recommended free resources as well as the occasional promotion of a product or program that would be of interest to your audience.

- **Ask about their needs and concerns.** Use questionnaires and get them involved. Ask them what they need and what they would most like to learn more about.

- **Send them an occasional gift.** It could be in the form of a free report, a relevant checklist, a chapter or two of your book, an audio recording, or access to a relevant video.

- **Share your knowledge.** When you impart something of value to your subscribers, they will see you as an educator, listen to what you have to say, and value their relationship with you.

- **Provide them with recommendations for products and services that can benefit them.** On occasion, provide your subscribers with information about products or services that you highly recommend and endorse. These can be products that you produce, free programs available online, or products on which you earn an affiliate commission.

Establish Yourself as an Authority

If you want to succeed in online marketing, you must be able to build strong credibility with your subscribers by establishing yourself as an authority on your topic.

Being an author of a published book gives you a high level of credibility all by itself. You can enhance your credibility by sharing your experiences. If you have a degree, have run a business, or have experience in marketing or other topics of interest to your audience, share this experience with them. You can also share feedback from satisfied clients. Let others tell your story and sing your praises, especially in the form of testimonials.

Another powerful way to build credibility is to share online videos and audios of you being interviewed. This will highlight your area of expertise and position you as an authority on the topic, due to your association with the person who is conducting the interview.

Build a Relationship with Your Readers Using Auto-Responder Messages

An auto-responder is a reliable way to get email delivered to a large group of people on a regular basis. You set up a welcome email to start and then you can decide how often you'd like your messages to go out. Auto-responders are a great way to educate customers and clients and build trust with your prospects. Automating your email communication will allow you to streamline your efforts and multiply your results.

In order for someone to receive your auto-responder messages, they need to subscribe to your list. They generally do this by filling out their name and email address via a form on your blog or website. By doing so, they are giving you permission to communicate with them. You can offer them something of value—such as an audio recording, a special report, or an eBook, on a topic they would be interested in—in exchange for their name and email address.

With an auto-responder service, you can either program the system so that when people opt-in, they are automatically added to your list, or you can select *the double opt-in method*. With this method, when someone signs up to receive your auto-responder messages, they will receive an email asking that they click a link to confirm their request to be added to your list. This is called a *double opt-in* and ensures that either you or someone else did not subscribe the reader without their permission. By requiring that your subscribers double opt-in, you also protect yourself from false spam reports by having a stored record of each person who has confirmed their subscription.

AWeber (www.WebmailConnections.com) is considered to be the most effective email marketing system on the Internet. They offer excellent customer support and training. Your account includes the ability to set up an unlimited number of lists, create online newsletters, broadcast your blog posts, and set up an attractive lead capture, opt-in form on your blog or website.

As you develop your list of subscribers, you will find that the more quality content you offer, the more people will remain on your list. If someone decides to unsubscribe, there is no reason to take it personally. It could be that he or she simply is receiving too much email and needs to streamline their communications.

If people know that the content they will be receiving from you can help them to grow their businesses, they will make it a priority to read what you send them. When composing your auto-responder messages, keep them brief, leave white space between paragraphs, make sure your subject lines are specific and personalized, and keep the number of requested action steps—such as visiting specific websites—to a minimum. These practices will increase the likelihood of your readers reading your messages and taking action.

The first thing you want to do is to create an initial message that welcomes your subscribers. A good rule of thumb is to reread your messages—by sending a test message to yourself—before you send it out to your list. As you read the message, put yourself in the shoes of your subscribers and give thought to how the message makes *you* feel.

Use your auto-responder service as a tool to *build relationships* with your prospects and clients; don't just focus on trying to "sell stuff." By taking the time to share valuable information and appreciation of your readers, you will create a loyal following and raving fans.

Common Mistakes to Avoid

If you want to build a solid relationship through email, you must be very careful **not** to commit these email marketing mistakes:

- **Spamming!** Never spam your email list. Even though they have given you permission to email them, that does not mean you should send them email on a daily basis. Learn to send email at strategic intervals.

- **Mailing to subscribers and followers only when you are selling something.** No one wants to be on your list if all you ever do is try to sell to him! The reason people join your mailing list is because they want something of value in exchange for being on your list. If they fail to see that value, they will unsubscribe.

- **Not keeping in regular contact with your list.**
This is the opposite of spamming. If you don't keep in touch with your subscribers on a regular basis, they will tend to forget who you are, and that can severely damage the relationship between you and your subscriber.

In a nutshell, building relationships is all about trust. The more people trust you, the easier it is for them to become your customer and to refer you to others. It may take a long time to build trust; but remember that trust can be shattered in a moment. Always put yourself in the shoes of your prospect or client and provide as much value as possible.

Relationship Marketing Using Greeting Cards

People do not want to be sold, but they do want to buy. The question to ask is why should they buy from you? By reaching out to your online customers and getting something into their hands from you, you have begun to build a deeper layer of relationship with these clients. Therefore, the likelihood of their becoming an ongoing customer is greatly increased. One of the most powerful things that you can do to set yourself apart and grow your business at the same time is to send a note of appreciation to your online customers, clients, and students. Imagine purchasing a book online and a few days later receiving an actual thank-you card, in the mail! The card has a picture of the book you purchased on the cover and on the inside of the card there is a smiling photo of the author thanking you for purchasing her book or participating in her workshop. What if the card also provided you with a few tips to prepare you for an upcoming program, thus maximizing your experience and your retention of the material? How would you feel about this author and how much more likely are you to participate more fully in her program?

As simple as that sounds, very few people will go the extra mile to put this type of system in place. Others might wonder why they should bother sending something through the mail when they can send something via email for free. My questions to you are, "What do you do with an email after you have read it?" and "What do you do with a heartfelt greeting card, especially one that includes a photograph, after you have read it?"

You may want to conduct a simple experiment to see what type of effect relationship marketing with greeting cards has on your business. Figure out how much it would cost you to send out a mailing through the post office to a segment of your list. Then, figure out how many sales you would need to generate in order to recoup your costs. Through this simple experiment, you will likely see that as both your client base and your income increase, there can also be a corresponding rise in referrals. Can you see what an impact this tiny gesture can have on your business and on your life?

Now obviously, you cannot send a card to everyone who purchases a book from you. Many of your customers will purchase your book from Amazon and you will not have access to their addresses. However, you can send cards to a selection of people who purchase your book from your website as well as those who enroll in workshops or coaching programs you offer. By doing this you will strengthen your relationships with your customers.

There is a wonderful service called SendOutCards (www.CardsYouRemember.com) that can help you automate the card sending process. While sending email to your subscribers relies on the use of an *online* auto-responder service, SendOutCards relies on an *offline* auto-responder service. With their online portal you can select a card or design a template, write your note, and click "send". Your card goes through the mail, with a stamp and your client receives that mailing in their hands.

They are going to take that card and put it up on their wall, their refrigerator, or on their computer and they're going to think about you a lot. This will increase the likelihood of this client purchasing from you again as well as referring you to others.

If the mailing you'll be sending out is to announce the launch of an upcoming program, related to the topic of your book, this would be a perfect opportunity for you to invite people to participate as well as to let them know how they can receive a referral commission by referring others.

Another type of mailing could be an unexpected, heartfelt card. This campaign is very easy to put in play and requires less than five minutes of your time each day. Consider creating a new practice of sending out a heartfelt card to one of your prospects, clients, colleagues, friends, or family members the first thing in the morning, each working day. By doing this before you even check your email, you will be creating a new and very powerful habit. Try doing this for just two weeks and notice the examples of positive impact—and perhaps even miracles—that come into your life.

There is nothing more powerful for building relationships than appreciating others. Within the coming week, consider reaching out to your warm market in one of the preceding ways.

There are many ways that you can touch people. Sending greeting cards is just one of them, but it sets you apart because your clients have something from you in their hands, which does not appear to sell them something. It is seen as appreciating them. By appreciating others, you are going to grow your business and sell more books.

Connecting with your audience via email and greeting cards are just two of the many marketing modalities available to you. In the following chapters you will discover additional relationship marketing strategies that will allow you to connect with your audience in a variety of ways.

Following each chapter you will find several key points listed. These will serve as a handy desk reference that you can refer to over and over again. Additionally, you will find a useful resource section, related to the topic of the chapter, which will provide you with easy access to tools and programs discussed in each chapter.

Keys to
Relationship Marketing Success

☛ Demonstrate that you care about people by focusing on building relationships *first* and making money *second.*

☛ Interact on the social networks by joining in the conversation. Become known as an expert in your field and someone who is willing to help others, the sales will follow.

☛ Grow your list of email subscribers and provide them with high quality content and useful information, at least once a week.

☛ Send cards, through the mail, to your prospects and clients to either educate or appreciate them. This will set you apart and make you memorable.

☛ Share videos and audios of you being interviewed. When people see and hear you, they will feel more connected to you and this will strengthen the relationship.

Relationship Marketing Resources

AWeber: www.WebmailConnections.com

Gmail: www.Gmail.com

iContact: www.iContact.com

SendOutCards: www.CardsYouRemember.com

Survey Monkey: www.SurveyMonkey.com

Vista Print: www.VistaPrint.com

Chapter Two:
Blogging for Authors

As an author, having a blog is essential to your online book marketing success. Your blog is the hub of your online world and provides you with a platform from which to share your message, sell your products, build community, house your membership site, show your videos, and share your knowledge. Your blog is not just where people go for content; it is where they go to connect with you. With your blog, you build community, you build credibility, and you create interaction.

Today's blog replaces the traditional website and offers you much more functionality and versatility. International blogging expert Yaro Starak shares that: *"A blog is a website with special powers."* While there are blog platforms available that will host your blog for free, the premiere blog platform—most widely used and recommended by successful marketers—is WordPress.org.

The basic difference between a free blogging platform and the premium WordPress.org platform (where the WordPress software is free but you pay for your hosting account and domain name) is analogous to the difference between renting and owning your own home. A free blogging platform has control of your online real estate and, at a moment's notice, could remove your site from their system. With a WordPress.org blog, you own your own domain and house your blog on your own hosting account. This provides you with complete control over your site, plus gives you the benefits of search engine rankings.

In this chapter I will share ways that you can use your blog to help you to promote your book and your brand. I will also provide you with an overview of the components of your blog and how to maximize the effectiveness of your site. To learn more about the actual installation of your blog, visit www.BloggingBasicsandBeyond.com or www.WordPress.org.

Your WordPress blog provides you with the features of a traditional website, but with much more functionality. You have easy and complete access to and control of your site along with a Web presence where people can learn about you, your interests, and your expertise.

Gone are the days when you needed to pay thousands of dollars to a Web master to create a website for you. Gone are the days when you needed to pay hundreds of dollars and wait days or weeks to have content changed on your site. With your WordPress website, you have complete control of both design and content.

A WordPress blog looks very much like a traditional website, is very user friendly, and it is a snap to add or change content. You simply click a button to get into the dashboard area where you are able to post an article, change a picture, or add an audio or a video as easily as it would be to create something in a Word document. It really is that easy and it gives you a lot of flexibility. Whenever you want to make a change to your blog, just log in, make the changes, click save, and the changes are instantly active on the site. The other major reason to use the WordPress blog platform, aside from the ease of use and control you have of your site, is that search engines love self-hosted WordPress blogs. With the blog platform, you are adding content on a regular basis and that is what search engines look for: fresh new content for their audience. To establish your blog as an authority site and to keep your viewers coming back regularly, you should post new content at least once a week; more often is even better.

You can encourage your readers to comment on your blog posts and begin an online conversation with them. You can also send out a tweet on Twitter or post a message on Facebook and let people know that you just posted an article on a given topic and that you'd value their feedback. Include a link to that actual post in order to get traffic to your site.

Why Do Authors Need a Blog

As an author, you want to become known as an expert in your field and an authority on your topic. Your blog provides you with a platform to share your message from. A blog allows you to easily have a Web presence where people can get to know you, come to like you and learn to trust you. By providing quality information you will create a base of thirsty learners and raving fans. This will allow you to grow both your business and your brand.

Your blog is a place where potential customers and publishers come to find out more about you and your book. Your blog provides you with a place to share your message and to share your work. You can have articles that you write in support of the material that you discuss in your book. You can share weekly tips or articles on the topic of your book, include audio clips from your book, as blog posts, post your interview and book tour schedules and much more.

Make your blog attractive and brand it with the colors of your business or your book. Display a video book trailer on the home page of your blog as that will invite people in and help them to make a connection with you.

Your blog also provides an easy way for people to purchase your book. You can sell your book directly from your site by providing a link to Amazon, as well as by offering special pricing or a special promotion for signed copies of your book.

The Anatomy of a Blog

Now that you know what a blog is, let's talk a bit about the various blog components. One of the most common questions I hear is, "What is the difference between a *blog post* and a *blog page?*" Another component of a blog that seems to mystify people is the use of *plugins*. Let me shed some light on these aspects of a WordPress blog so that you can gain a better understanding and become better equipped to begin posting articles and using plugins on your own blog.

Post versus Page

A *post* is an article that shows up on your blog page along with other posts. You may have noticed that when content is posted to a blog, the most current post is at the top of the page and older posts move down the page over time.

Let's say you write on the topic of natural health and you want to post a variety of articles over the course of weeks or months. You can have all of those articles labeled within a category called natural health. Every time you create a new post and you click that it belongs to the category of natural health, it is going to show up on the post page and it is also going to show up when your readers click on the category link to "natural health," along with all the other posts on that topic.

A *page* is different from a post because a page is static, meaning that the content does not change every time you create a blog post. The content on your pages only changes when you intentionally add or remove content. A page on a blog is similar to a traditional website page.

The exception to this is the *blog page*. This is the page where your blog posts will be displayed. On the blog page, you will typically see a mini synopsis and an image for each post. You can click to view the full article or you can scroll down the page to look at other blog post topics. If you want to read more on any post, you can click on the title or on the "read more" tag to access the full article.

Theme

Your blog theme is the "clothing" for your site. Changing a theme is as easy as changing your shirt or coat. You can either use the theme that comes with WordPress, or you can purchase a premium blog theme. The theme that comes with WordPress is attractive and clean looking, yet it is plain and does not come with additional support.

When you purchase a premium theme, you typically have access to an active and responsive forum where you can easily get the answers to your questions. I recommend the Studio Press themes for several reasons. I have been using these themes since 2005 and am continually impressed with the high level of customer support and consistent upgrades to keep up with the evolution of the WordPress platform. There are many themes to choose from and they are easily customizable. If you'd like to take a look at their collection, visit: www.ThemesbyStudioPress.com

Permalinks

Permalinks refers to the permanent link to your individual WordPress posts. When WordPress is first installed on your website the permalinks typically consist of your URL followed by fancy characters and numbers. You can easily change the permalinks to ones that include your URL followed by the title of the article, which is more search engine friendly than the default settings.

When you install WordPress, the default settings for the permalinks are activated. You want to set up a custom structure so that it shows the domain name plus the title of the article. You do this by clicking on "Custom Structure" from the Permalinks section on your WordPress dashboard. Next add the following code in the space provided: /%postname%/. When you do this your new URL will look like this: http://YourDomain.com/name-of-post

Widgets

A blog widget is in essence a text or code placeholder which extends the functionality of your blog. Typically widgets are located on your blog's sidebar though premium blog themes often have the capability to also add widgets to your home page. Widgets can house the code for your opt-in form which people can use to subscribe to your email list. You also have access to widgets that display images, links to your posts, pages or external sites, your Twitter feed, your Facebook fan page, your Networked Blogs followers, and more.

Opt-In Form

Your opt-in form can be displayed in a widget on your blog's sidebar. Your auto-responder service will provide you with the code needed to create this opt-in form. AWeber, for example, provides you with a wide variety of designs to choose from. This will allow you to carry your branded design through to your opt-in form.

Plugins

A *plugin* is essentially a piece of software that extends the functionality of your site. Most plugins are free, but you need to be selective in your use of plugins. There are thousands to choose from and they will slow down your site if you add too many or could conflict with other plugins. If you are interested in finding out more about WordPress plugins visit www.PowerfulPlugins.com or www.WordPress.org/extend/plugins.

RSS Feed

RSS stands for "really simple syndication". Your readers can subscribe to your RSS feed and have easy access to your blog posts from their computer. They can elect to have announcements sent to them via email, or they can access your RSS feed via a reader, such as Google Reader. Google Reader provides a convenient way to view all of your RSS feed subscriptions from one easy location.

Now You Are Ready to Blog

Now that your blog is set up and you know your way around your site, you can begin posting content. Establish a regular writing schedule and put a system in place for keeping track of ideas for future articles. The best blog posts are narrow in scope, useful, and informative.

Encourage your readers to post comments by asking compelling questions, or asking for their opinion, at the end of your posts.

10 Things to Blog About

1. Share an update about a recent book reading or interview you have participated in.

2. Comment on another blog post or comment, on your blog.

3. Comment on a news event and on how it relates to your field.

4. Write a how-to post.

5. Tell an entertaining and educational story, related to your topic.

6. Address common frustrations in your industry.

7. Compose a detailed, step-by-step tutorial on how to do something that your blog readers would benefit from.

8. Invite an expert in your field to share his or her insights and wisdom with your readers.

9. Make a list of FAQs (frequently asked questions) that will appeal to your target audience. What are common questions people have and what are your answers?

10. Review a book on your topic area and share your opinions on what the author has to say.

If you have exhausted this list, visit some of your favorite blogs for inspiration. Keep an ongoing list of topics you'd like to blog about and you will never be at a loss for new material.

Promoting Your Blog and Generating Online Traffic

Creating a blog and writing a few posts every week isn't going to help you sell more books unless you also work at promoting your blog. Online blog marketing opportunities abound, and most of them are free. Make use of every chance you get to find new followers and get links back to your blog posts. Here are some easy ways to promote your blog:

- Begin using social media outlets such as Facebook, Twitter, and LinkedIn. Automate announcements of new blog posts by using the "Twitter Tools" plugin on your blog and the "Networked Blogs" application on Facebook. This will automatically submit new blog posts to such sites every time you post. Doing so is an important way to gain new readers and subscribers.

- Add a "like" widget to your blog. Facebook offers a widget that allows people to click on a link, follow your blog, and then be notified of new posts. Followers then show up on your sidebar, if you choose, and show other visitors how popular you are.

- Submit your blog to blog directories. There are dozens of good sites which allow you to submit your blog, description, and link for free. When readers find a blog they are interested in, they can visit or subscribe to new posts. Google the term "blog directories" for a list of possibilities.

- Use every post to invite readers to subscribe or follow. Add a *footer* to your posts that says something to the effect of, "Enjoy this article? Receive email alerts when new articles are available! Just click on the *follow* button or subscribe above."

- Seek out guest bloggers to post to your blog, and when you use one of their posts, ask that guest blogger to help promote it by tweeting to his followers and posting a link on his blog. This approach gives your audience exposure to a wider range of topics and lines of thought. It also induces reciprocity, as other bloggers will likely want to have you become a guest blogger.

- Become a guest blogger. Offer other bloggers and website owners high-quality articles in exchange for a link from their site to your site.

- Add a line below your email signature with a link back to your blog. Every time someone reads one of your email messages, you'll be advertising your blog.

- Use quality search engine optimization (SEO) strategies in your blog description and in every post you write. Use your keywords in the title and throughout your post. This way, you will get better search engine results when people search for the topic(s) you write about.

- Post comments on other blogs. You will have the opportunity to provide a link back to your blog when you fill out the requested information in the "comments" box. This commenting strategy works especially well on blogs that are frequented by your target audience and the professionals who serve them. You will quickly become known as an authority on your topic.

- Respond to comments! Authors who respond to comments generally get a lot more comments than those who ignore their readers.

- Use social media to promote your blog posts. Announce your new posts on Twitter, Facebook, LinkedIn, and other social media sites. WordPress and other blogging platforms have widgets that will automatically tweet your new posts or post them to Facebook and other sites.

The more ways you can find to promote your blog online, the more visitors, readers, subscribers, and followers you'll get. *That means the more people you'll reach with your message and that is the whole idea of writing a blog in the first place.*

Ways to Promote Your Blog Offline

- **Business cards.** Include your blog URL on your business cards and share them generously. Give your cards out to people you meet and mention your blog to them.

- **Talk about your blog.** Promoting your blog offline is just a matter of mentioning your latest work as often as is appropriate. When you are excited about what you are doing, you will find a way to work it into conversations!

- **Attend network meetings**. When you go to Chamber of Commerce and other local networking groups, promote your blog as your main contact point.

- **Print handouts.** Create a free print version of a favorite blog post or two to hand at networking events. Make sure to include your blog address at the bottom of the page.

- **Write**. Submit an article or press release to your local newspaper, an industry magazine, or print newsletter.

Whether you are promoting your blog online or offline, finding new followers does require some work, but it is well worth the effort in terms of added exposure for your blog and book. You will get added sales as you convert those new followers into clients or customers.

By now, you should see blogging as an integral part of your online book marketing strategy. As with any promotional technique, though, blogging is not a "one and done" proposition. Instead, it will be a task you will need to invest in over and over again. However, that investment will pay off in long-term dividends. Long after you write the post or record the video, that little piece of you will be waiting for your readers, prospects, and customers, showing them who you are and what you have to offer.

In the next chapter you will discover social networking strategies to increase your reach. With your blog as the hub of your online book marketing empire, your social networks are the spokes from which information and idea travels. You can automate announcements to go out from your blog to the social networks whenever a new post has been added. You can also mention and provide links directly to your blog, from the social networks.

In addition to the Big Four social networks, you will learn about social networks that are designed specifically for authors. Focus on building relationships and sharing relevant information and your network and your book sales will grow.

Keys to
Blogging Success

᭴ Your blog is the hub of your online empire. Create
an attractive, interactive environment where people
will want to visit often.

᭴ Set up the Twitter Tools plugin so that it
automatically publishes an announcement each time
you post a new article on your blog.

᭴ Add an opt-in form to the sidebar on your blog and
offer your visitors a useful gift in exchange for their
name and email address.

᭴ Add a welcome video on the home page of your blog.
This will captivate viewers and give them the
opportunity to connect with you. They will then
spend more time exploring your site.

᭴ Interact with your blog readers by encouraging
comments and responding back when people leave
comments. By doing so you will encourage additional
comments and interaction on your site.

Blogging Resources

aWeber:	www.WebmailConnections.com
Elegant Themes:	www.ElegantThemes.com
Free Blog Factory:	www.BuildMyBlogPlease.com
GoDaddy:	www.BestDomainPricing.com
Gravatar:	www.Gravatar.com
Host Gator:	www.WebHostingGator.com
Networked Blogs:	www.NetworkedBlogs.com
Powerful Plugins:	www.PowerfulPlugins.com
Studio Press:	www.ThemesbyStudioPress.com
The Blog Station:	www.TheBlogStation.com
Wishlist:	www.WishlistMembershipPlugin.com
WordPress:	www.WordPress.org

Chapter Three:
Social Networking for Authors

Social networking is a powerful way to grow your business, reach, readers, and sales. As an author, you want to become known for your area of expertise and as the go-to person for your topic. The purpose of social networking is not to constantly promote your book, but rather to be seen as someone who interacts and offers value to the community.

You want to network with people who are interested in you and your topic as well as with other authors. By networking with other authors you will gain ideas and suggestions for additional ways to promote your book. Networking with people interested in the topic you write about allows you to grow your readership as well as the sales of your books and programs. *Engage your readers in conversations that lead to more referrals and sales.*

Social media sites offer an excellent opportunity to let other people know that you have a book, and that you are available for speaking engagements. Much of this networking can be set up to run on autopilot by linking your blog to the social networks with a Twitter notification plugin called Twitter Tools. It is easy to set up and, then, each time you publish a new article to your blog, you will be sending out a notification, or tweet, to Twitter. To access the Twitter Tools plugin, visit: www.WordPress.org/extend/plugins/twitter-tools.

You can also activate settings on Facebook and LinkedIn to display your tweets from Twitter, thus automatically notifying all three networks each time an article is posted. To take things even further, you can install the Ezine Articles plugin on your WordPress blog. As a result, each time you post to your blog, your article is automatically uploaded to Ezine Articles. To access this plugin, go to the author tools section of your dashboard at EzineArticles.com.

By taking the time to set up your profile on several of the key networks, you will benefit in many ways. You will meet and connect with more people and become known as an authority on your topic. You will also gain exposure to people who are looking for speakers or people to interview, as they will have greater access to you. You will also benefit from additional links to your blog, as you are able to list links on your social networking profiles.

There are thousands of social networks to choose from and the thought of that could be a bit overwhelming. To keep things simple, focus first on the Big Four social networks: Facebook, LinkedIn, Twitter, and YouTube. From there you can explore social networks designed specifically with authors in mind. I've listed some of my favorite author networks later on in this chapter.

As you go through this material, think about which networks are most appealing to you. Take time each week to explore a new network. It does not take long to set up your profile and, if you stop by at least once a week or so, you will be able to add new content and interact with the other members.

Tips for Enhancing Your Social Networking Profiles and Experience

- Brand yourself across the social networks, whenever possible, by using the same profile ID and photograph. Your profile ID can represent your name, your book, your topic, or your product.

- Create a professional-looking profile with a professional headshot photo of yourself. Make sure to select a photo where you are smiling, as this makes a positive impact and draws people to you.

- Schedule fifteen minutes several times a week—as well as one longer, weekly session—to interact on your social networks.

- Join a few groups on topics of interest to you, ask questions, and participate in discussions.

- Set up your signature to include your book title, subtitle, and Web address.

- Consider setting your email preferences so that the bulk of the messages from your social networks stay on the network and are not sent to your email box. This allows you to focus on these messages when you have scheduled time for social networking.

- Sell people on you, not on your business. Build relationships and be of help to others.

Grow Your Social-Networking Presence

You can grow a vibrant, social-networking presence in as little as fifteen minutes, several times per week. The trick is to schedule this time in your calendar. If you don't, you may find that 1) you either never seem to get around to networking online or that 2) you end up spending way too much time on the social networks, thus taking time away from writing and other key book marketing activities. By scheduling your social networking time, you'll stay focused and you'll prioritize this time. Following are a few activities to choose from:

- Visit your social networks.

- Check your network inbox messages.

- Post a status update in which you share something about yourself or something that you are working on. Do this in a way that will create interest and not sound like a sales pitch.

- Visit one or more of your groups and comment on discussions.

- Visit the website of someone you've been interacting with and comment about his or her work or something you have in common.

- Begin a discussion topic and encourage others to chime in.

I have found that I get more responses when I share something interesting but not too personal. For example, when I've shared about a great book I read or course that I took, people generally comment back and join in the conversation. I also find that when I share something humorous I get the most responses.

As an example, I came across a (fictitious) video that featured an application for a cell phone that translates animal languages. On Facebook, I got many comments from people thanking me for the chuckle or commenting on ideas for other clever gadgets. This type of information is a conversation starter and something that makes people smile.

The "Big Four" Social Networks

Facebook: www.Facebook.com

Facebook is the top (most widely used) social network in the world. You have the opportunity to connect easily with new friends, locate old friends and colleagues, share photographs and videos, syndicate your blog content via your RSS feed, and create pages which can focus on your brand, your book, or your products. Be sure to use a professional photograph for your profile. Set up a fan page and brand it with your image or logo. Take care to name your page as an extension of your brand.

Create a Facebook Fan Page for Your Book

Facebook allows you to create a customized page for your fans to "like." You can include pictures, text links, videos, and many other pertinent applications. Your Facebook fan page is no different than other social media platforms. You can promote your events; share engaging content with your readers; and through regular status updates, you can share interesting facts about your industry. You can also integrate your blog posts by pulling in your RSS feed, as well as publish informative videos and articles that will position you as an expert within your industry.

Create a fan page that is focused specifically on your book. You can program the RSS feed from your book blog to automatically post an image and excerpt from each of your blog posts. This option will create interest in your book and provide you with yet another way to connect with your readers and fans. You can also post announcements and invitations to online and offline events.

Be sure to post status updates to this fan page at least once a week. You may want to schedule this as a recurring appointment in your calendar. It will allow you the opportunity to not only update your fan page with pertinent content, but to interact with your readers.

It is vital that you interact with your fans. We are in the midst of a marketing revolution that revolves around building and sustaining relationships. Therefore, it is vital that you participate in the discussion, answer questions, and take the time to engage with your fans on a regular basis.

Facebook fan pages have been refined and offer incredible opportunities for connecting with your audience and driving traffic to any Web page you'd like people to visit. You may want to bring people to your book blog, your book listing on Amazon, a video, or elsewhere.

To find out more about Facebook fan pages, visit Facebook.com and scroll to the bottom of the page to access the "help" section as well as Fanpage Engine at: www.AuthorsMarketingCircle.com/fanpageengine.

Networked Blogs

Networked Blogs (www.NetworkedBlogs.com) provides you with another way to import your blog feed to Facebook, so that your fan page is automatically updated every time you post to your blog. Of course, fans are then able to read and comment on your blog post directly on your fan page.

Twitter: www.Twitter.com

Twitter is a social network that provides a platform to communicate your (up to) 140-character messages—known as tweets—to the world. It is considered a micro-blog, as you are constantly adding new content. The restriction of using only 140 characters enables you to be unique with your message. Some may find this aspect challenging; but when you are able to perfect it to a point where you are not sounding like a salesperson, your audience will grow.

The types of messages that people respond to most readily are tweets that make them smile, think, or feel.

For the most part share thought-provoking and conversation-provoking comments. Occasionally share news about your upcoming teleseminar or event. As an author, you can also thank a specific person for his or her Amazon book review and provide a link to the review for people to enjoy.

Begin by customizing your profile page. Select a user name that identifies you or relates to your business. The next step is to click on the "settings" tab and customize your profile and preferences. Be sure to list your Web or blog address so that anyone who goes to your Twitter page can quickly access your site. You will also want to add a description about your business and upload your photo.

Next, choose one of several background themes or upload a custom theme, thus setting you apart and creating interest. You can choose to have notices sent to your email address or not. In today's busy world, with so much email, you may elect *not* to receive notices via email but rather make a point of checking your messages when you log into your Twitter account.

Now that you have your account set up, you will want to begin following other Twitter accounts and focus on getting followers. One thing you can do is allow Twitter to search your Gmail or Yahoo! email accounts to see whether anyone in your address book has already registered an account on Twitter. From that same screen, you can send out an invitation to anyone in your address book to join you on Twitter.

There are a couple of ways to get followers. One is to add a badge or widget on your blog or website, inviting people to follow you on Twitter. Another way to gain followers is to find other Twitter accounts within your niche by searching keywords on Twitter or at search.twitter.com. Follow the people who are following them. Many of those people will follow you back.

Now that you have a list of followers, you can begin tweeting messages. In addition to inviting people to stop by your blog or website, consider tweeting links to interesting articles or sites that you've discovered. Make sure that your tweets are of value or people will stop following you just as fast as they followed you. No one wants to receive numerous "buy my stuff" messages.

Automate Your Twitter Tweets

You can automate your Twitter feed to show up as status updates on Facebook. This gives you a wider reach and maximizes your time and effort. By activating the Facebook Application Programming Interface (API) to allow Twitter updates, your tweets will automatically show up on both Twitter and Facebook. You can also program your Twitter feed to show up on LinkedIn.

Make Twitter Relevant

As a professional, it is essential that you tweet about things that are relevant to your topic and your book. When people view your Twitter feed, do you want them to know what you had for breakfast or do you want them to know about your latest book reading or blog post?

The people who are clearly adding value, giving tips, and pointing others to articles and interesting books will be the ones who grow their followings and enhance their statuses as experts. Be really clear about why you are on the social networks and what your message is. If you are writing a book on recipes, then obviously you want to talk about new recipes that you discover. If your topic focus is on boating, then you want to be talking about boats and boating. What do you want to be known for? That is what you want to discuss and share information on.

Streamline Your Twitter Experience with HootSuite

HootSuite (www.HootSuite.com) provides you with an online user interface that allows you to streamline your Twitter experience and be able to more easily communicate with others on Twitter. You can create tabs and columns to organize your social networks into friends, news, search terms, keyword tracking, and more. You can also create a stream that displays a list of all tweets where your name is mentioned, as well as the names of anyone you want to keep up with. This is a powerful way to keep a pulse on the conversations taking place on Twitter.

Within each tab, you are able to create up to six streams. You can also schedule your tweets and have them appear when you want them to. Provide rich, nourishing content to your followers at any time of day using the HootSuite tweet scheduler.

LinkedIn: www.LinkedIn.com

The LinkedIn network is another essential component to your social networking strategy. On LinkedIn, you have the ability to share a great deal of information about yourself, including your background, accomplishments, education, and much more. You can set up an online resume on LinkedIn. I have been contacted by people wanting to do business with me as a result of the professional quality of my LinkedIn profile.

LinkedIn has a wide variety of interest groups in which you can participate. The best strategy is to join fewer groups in order to participate more often. You may also choose to start a group, which is a great way to market your name and brand as well as share your expertise. Consider creating a buzz around the topics of conversation that your target market and you are interested in.

Search and find the groups that either you are interested in or your target market will be involved in and join those in order to position your name and brand for more exposure.

LinkedIn gives you the opportunity to add different applications to your profile page, such as videos or PowerPoint presentations. There is also a way to ask for testimonials from your contacts, which will be made public to those who visit your profile page. The main purpose of LinkedIn and any other social network is to build connections and ultimately relationships. Each network has a different platform and method of approaching this goal, but all are great avenues to build your brand and name.

Get involved in discussions and people will take note. Be a giver, offer ideas and suggestions, and make introductions when you are able to do so.

YouTube: www.YouTube.com

YouTube is the number one video-sharing site in the world! It is also one of the most visited websites in the world and is considered to be the second most accessed search engine in the world, second only to Google. When people want to learn something, they can simply go to YouTube and look it up, the way many of us used to look for answers to our questions in an encyclopedia.

YouTube is also considered to be a premiere social networking site because it allows you to find and follow other YouTube members. This is a great way to grow your network and your reach as you can connect with people who have subscribed to or who are following channels that you are interested in. At the same time, people who are interested in a specific topic will find you as a subscriber or follower on topics that interest them.

YouTube easily allows you to upload videos, display information and Web links, create a branded YouTube channel, and create playlists on any topic you'd like. YouTube also allows videos to be embedded on other sites. By simply copying the embedding code, people can share your video on their websites. This feature will allow you to expand your reach and have more people see your videos.

A fantastic way to gain exposure for your book is to create book trailers, book reviews, and book excerpts in video and upload them to your YouTube account. As you upload your videos, you have the opportunity to assign tags and keywords to your videos. This additional feature will make them easier to find when people are searching for content on your topic.

The first thing you want to do is to set up a channel on YouTube. You can carry over your branded image when selecting the colors and background for your channel. As you create videos, you can upload them to YouTube and post them on your blog. There are some very powerful things that you can do with your YouTube videos, such as add text and callouts.

You want to have a branded YouTube station where you can display your photo or logo. You can also create a user ID that represents your brand. People can view your videos on YouTube and they can also embed them on their own websites, thus giving you even more exposure. Having a YouTube channel is a great way to grow your reach and your followers.

Top Social Networks for Authors

In addition to the Big Four, you will find that there are social networks that are designed specifically for authors. Take time to explore each of these sites.

Author Central on Amazon:
> www.AuthorCentral.Amazon.com

Author Central is, a free service that Amazon offers so that authors can gain more exposure and promote their books. At Author Central, you can share with your readers the most current information about yourself, your events, and your work. In addition, you can view and edit your bibliography, add a photo and biography to a personal profile, upload book cover images and videos, track your book sales, and pull in the RSS feed from you blog as a way to connect with readers.

AuthorNation:
> www.AuthorNation.com

AuthorNation provides a creative atmosphere where writers, poets, published authors, and enthusiastic readers can connect. If you are a published author interested in networking with other skilled writers and promoting your books, or a reader searching for a good story, you will want to explore AuthorNation.

Authors Den:
> www.AuthorsDen.com

AuthorsDen is one of the largest and most vibrant online literary communities for both authors and potential readers. Nearly 1.5 million readers a month visit this website and have the opportunity to review books while interacting with others.

BlogTalkRadio:
www.BlogTalkRadio.com

BlogTalkRadio allows you to host a live Internet radio talk show with just your telephone and computer. BlogTalkRadio has tens of thousands of hosts and millions of listeners tuning in and joining the conversation.

CinchCast:
www.Cinchcast.com

CinchCast allows members to create and share audio messages and recordings. Using their simple interface, you are able to produce and broadcast your recordings through Facebook, Twitter, CinchCast.com, and other social networks.

FiledBy:
www.FiledBy.com

FiledBy is a comprehensive directory of authors and contributors who showcase themselves and their work. FiledBy is also a place where readers can discover and connect with authors and buy their books.

Good Reads:
www.GoodReads.com

GoodReads claims to be "the largest social network for readers in the world." They have more than 4,100,000 members who have added more than 110,000,000 books to their GoodReads bookshelves. GoodReads members recommend books, compare what they are reading, keep track of what they've read and would like to read, form book clubs, and interact with others.

Redroom:

> www.Redroom.com

Red Room is a great place to discuss and buy books, discover books, and join in the conversation. Members can upload pictures, videos, and other media files and socialize and connect with readers, published and aspiring writers, publishers, agents, students, researchers, and other publishing and literary professionals.

Shelfari:

> www.Shelfari.com

Shelfari is known as a gathering place for authors, aspiring authors, publishers, and readers. They have numerous features to enable these groups to connect in an enjoyable way.

Squidoo:

> www.Squidoo.com

Squidoo is a micro blogging community developed by Seth Godin. Members can create "lenses" online. Lenses are Web pages that allow you to gather everything you know about your topic and *"snap it all into focus"*. Squidoo provides members with the opportunity to share interests, build their online identity and credibility, and connect with new readers and friends. Authors use Squidoo for book promotion by creating lenses for their books where they can share multimedia content and provide links to their works on Amazon.com.

You Publish:

> www.YouPublish.com

YouPublish is a marketplace for publishing and consuming digital files. You can create single or multi-file publications and then charge for them or make them available for free. While all of the files they host are easily downloadable, they've gone the extra mile to provide file players for common file formats, allowing your fans and customers access to your publications directly from the YouPublish website.

Time to Take Action

Now that you have an overview of the Big Four social networks as well as specific social networks, designed specifically for authors, it is time to take action. Remember to use the same, professionally looking, photo on each network you register for and select a username that ties in with your branding.

In the first three chapters of this book we explored ways to develop the foundation of your online platform. In the following chapters we will be exploring a variety of ways to create and deliver your content and share the message of your book. Remember to refer to the "keys" at the end of each chapter and be sure to print out the Quickstart Guide, listed at the back of this book, so that you have a handy desk reference, easily accessible.

Keys to Social Networking Success

- Set up your profile on at least two of the Big Four social networks. Take care to add the same, professional looking, photo so that you have a branded image across the networks.
- Visit the key social networks, recommended for authors in this chapter, and pick one or two to join.
- Join a group on LinkedIn and participate in the conversation at least once a week. By giving, not selling, you can become known as an expert in your field. Build relationships and be of help to others.
- Create a Facebook fan page, for your book, and add the RSS feed from your blog so that every time you post a new article, it shows up on your fan page.
- Schedule fifteen minutes, several times a week, to interact on the social networks. By scheduling this time, you will make it a priority and by keeping to your allotted time, you will be able to complete the other tasks on your schedule.

Social Networking Resources

Author Central:	www.AuthorCentral.Amazon.com
AuthorNation:	www.AuthorNation.com
Authors Den:	www.AuthorsDen.com
BlogTalkRadio:	www.BlogTalkRadio.com
CinchCast:	www.Cinchcast.com
Facebook:	www.Facebook.com
FiledBy:	www.FiledBy.com
Good Reads:	www.GoodReads.com
HootSuite:	www.HootSuite.com
LinkedIn:	www.LinkedIn.com
Networked Blogs:	www.NetworkedBlogs.com
Redroom:	www.Redroom.com
Shelfari:	www.Shelfari.com
Squidoo:	www.Squidoo.com
Twitter:	www.Twitter.com
You Publish:	www.YouPublish.com

Chapter Four:
Promote Your Book and Your Message with Teleseminars

As an author, providing additional ways for your audience to connect with you and hear the message of your book will grow your business and increase your book sales. Teleseminars provide you with a platform to reach and connect with your audience.

Teleseminars also provide you with the raw material to create additional books as well as a wide variety of other products and programs. From audio recordings—which can be sold as downloads or CDs—to an eCourse or eBook created from audio transcripts, the possibilities are seemingly endless.

A powerful way to connect with your audience and build a relationship is to provide them with ways to hear your voice, your enthusiasm, and your message. This will give them a sense of who you are and provide a way for them to get to know you. Offering teleseminars is an extremely effective way to accomplish this goal.

What is a Teleseminar?

A teleseminar is a seminar conducted over a telephone as a conference call. On your teleseminar, you can either speak via a muted line—thus cutting out all background noise—or you can allow audience participation or questions by individuals as well as participation by one or more guest speakers.

Teleseminars are a fantastic way for you to share your expertise with a large group of people at one time. For those not able to attend the live call, you can create an MP3 recording of your teleseminar. Therefore, people have the option of listening online or downloading the recording to their computers.

Teleseminars can be delivered on any topic. They can be interactive or presented as a lecture or seminar. Teleseminars are very effective in getting your message out to solve the challenges that your audience is facing and for you to become a well-known expert in your field.

These sessions can be one-time events or a series of calls. They can be free or you can charge for them. You can allow free attendance to the live event and charge for the replay. You can structure the offering in any number of ways. One popular model is where you offer a teleseminar series with four or five modules, delivered once or twice a week, or in a concentrated period over the course of a week.

You can provide a workbook or study guide for the attendees, so that they retain the information better and are more attentive. These types of teleseminars can be very profitable and are invaluable as a source of content that you can repurpose into a wide variety of additional information products.

As an author, teleseminars provide you with a powerful way to:

- Share the message of your book and develop a following.

- Provide a platform for a book study program.

- Teach a course based on the content of your book.

- Offer group phone coaching sessions.

Teleseminars are by far one of the best tools that you can use to gain mass visibility in a very cost-effective way. You can invite people to attend an information session, and then at the end of the teleseminar, invite them to go to a specific website where, as an example, they can obtain a free report, a chapter of your book, or an audio of you being interviewed. They then opt-in to your mailing list in exchange for your gift and you begin to build a relationship with them. The more you gain visibility as an author, the easier it is to sell your books because people like to buy books from authors they consider to be celebrities or leading experts within an industry.

At first thought, the idea of holding your own teleseminar might seem as out-of-reach as opening your own chain of restaurants. However, as you will discover in this chapter, that is simply not the case. Teleseminars are not just for the celebrities such as Tony Robbins, John Grey, and Suze Orman. In fact, thousands of authors, coaches, Internet marketers, small business owners, and solo entrepreneurs regularly use teleseminars to reach new audiences, establish themselves as experts, and create new products, and so can you.

Teleseminars are a lot like traditional, in-person seminars, except that they are typically less formal and presented over a teleconference or bridge line rather than in person, at a physical location.

It is easy to see the advantages of teleseminars. You won't have to limit yourself to the number of people you can round up and lure into a hotel room or lecture hall. Instead, you can draw your audience from all over the globe and connect with them by phone.

Teleseminars do not have to be mysterious or complicated. In fact, any time you are on the phone, talking about your books, products, services, or on anything related to marketing your business, you are conducting a teleseminar. Of course, you can also host teleseminars that are more formal and require more planning and care in execution.

In this chapter, I am going to cover the basics of teleseminars:

1. Why you should incorporate teleseminars into your book marketing mix.

2. How you should set them up and promote them for best results.

3. How you can leverage the power of what you have created.

In a matter of days, you could be producing top-notch teleseminars that grow your business, your book sales, and your bottom line.

What Can Teleseminars Do for You?

With the ready availability of low-cost (or no-cost) long-distance service and conference call lines, teleseminars have become increasingly popular. Instead of spending thousands of dollars traveling to give an in-person presentation, you can meet your customers and prospects right where they are, anywhere in the world. Here's what you can do with teleseminars:

- Present an introduction to your book.

- Provide a book study course.

- Introduce new products.

- Get known in a new market, and get to know that market in turn.

- Interview experts and share their knowledge with your audience.

- Answer questions about your area of expertise.

In addition, teleseminars can help you do the following:

- **Sell more.** By presenting a sales presentation over the phone, you offer much more interactivity and a stronger personal connection than you can by advertising on your website or via a direct mail piece.

- **Create products.** The calls themselves can be turned into products or classes. You can sell access to your live events, or you can record them and sell them later as CDs or audio downloads, and much more.

- **Generate content for your next book.** You can also create the content of your next book by having someone interview you on a series of prioritized questions that you provide. Go into as much depth as possible on each question, have the recording transcribed, and then go to work editing the content of your new book.

- **Get to know your audience.** Being able to interact with your audience in real time allows an unprecedented level of market research, right in the moment.

- **Establish yourself.** If you interview experts in your topic area, you will quickly be seen as an expert by association.

- **Build your list.** Teleseminars are popular ways to introduce yourself to a new market. It is easy to invite people to your free events and, as they sign up, they become part of your list.

- **Create trust.** Trust is crucial when you want to do business online, and one of the best ways to build trust with your audience is to interact with them directly. As they hear your voice live on the call and, as they ask questions and get answers right then and there, you become "real" to them and they will be able to bond with you. This is something that is much harder to accomplish through sales letters and emails.

- **Develop your teleseminar skills.** The best way to learn is by doing. The information in this chapter will provide you with the knowledge to begin hosting your own teleseminars, immediately.

Planning for Success

In order to pull off a great teleseminar, you will need to plan for success. Surely, there are things that can go wrong; but, if you plan your teleseminar well, most potential challenges can be avoided. Let's review the four steps you need to do to ensure your teleseminar will go as smoothly as possible:

1. Start by brainstorming a list of possible topics for your teleseminar. When it comes to scope, ideal topics are suitable for magazine articles rather than books! In short, go through your list of topics and decide for each one whether it is so broad you'd need a book to cover it, or if you could do it justice in a magazine article. Then, make a list of your top choices. Be sure to select a topic you feel comfortable with.

In addition to speaking on a topic in your area of expertise, you could host a teleseminar where, for example, you answer the top questions your book addresses or those your readers most frequently ask.

2. Choose a good topic. Choosing a topic for your teleseminar is much like choosing a topic for a blog post. You do not want something too broad, or you will have no focus. You do not want something too narrow, or you will run out of things to say. Instead, you want to balance your need to cover new ground with your need to keep the length and breadth of your teleseminar manageable. For your first go-round, I suggest keeping things tight and focused. You should also plan to keep your call to an hour or so.

3. Pick a date and time. Next, you need to pick a date and time. Rather than trying to find a day and time that works for everyone in your target audience, pick a date and time that works best for you and one that you feel would be convenient for people in your target audience. Realize that no matter what you do, you simply won't be able to pick a time that is convenient for everyone! Instead, pick a time that works for you, and go with it. You can always make the audio available later, if you like.

4. Decide on whether to charge or not. Are you planning to charge for your teleseminar? You will want to decide upfront whether to charge or not and whether you should offer upsells such as the MP3 recording and transcripts. In a later section, we're going to cover fee versus no fee teleseminars in more detail.

That's it! These are the key decisions you need to make before you get started. Keep in mind that these are not necessarily either/or decisions. There are a range of options you can select from, so let's discuss those in greater detail.

Prepare for Your First Teleseminar

For your first teleseminar, you may want to simply invite some friends or family members to attend. Deliver your message while live people are on the call with you. There's something very powerful about delivering your message to a live audience that you cannot capture when you are recording at home by yourself. When you have attendees with you on the call, you cannot say, "Wait a minute. Let me rewind that." As any entertainer knows, a live audience brings out the best in the performer. This causes you to keep moving forward and sharing your message. You can always edit the audio recording and the transcripts afterwards. Once you have done this a few times, you will be a pro. You will get more comfortable as time goes on.

Remember, we are a busy society and people have full schedules. The flexibility of the teleseminar format allows audience members to listen to the call live or afterwards via the recording. If people are not able to attend your live call, you should never take it personally. People have busy schedules. Make the content as accessible as possible for as many people as possible in as many ways as possible.

Make it easy for your audience to access your material. Let them know ahead of time that they will have access to the live call, as well as the call recording, so they can listen in at a time that is most convenient for them. Another great way to share your message is by podcasting your teleseminars on iTunes. This is very easy to do and you can choose whether to offer your content for free or whether you want to charge people to download it from iTunes.

By making the recording accessible to your audience after the call, you make it easy for them to consume and absorb the content. Some people will listen online, while others will download the recording to their iPod or burn a CD to listen to in the car. The more ways you can get your content into the hands of your audience, the better off you are. This gives your audience greater access to your knowledge and products and gives you the opportunity for building stronger relationships with them.

Pricing Options

Should you charge for your teleseminars? If so, how much? That depends on your goals. If your main purpose is to promote a product or service—or to build your audience—you may decide to offer your expertise for free, thereby maximizing the number of people who participate.

The benefits of hosting a free teleseminar are:

- You will get more registrations.

- It is easier to implement. You won't have to worry about processing payments or integrating a shopping cart with your sales page or email service.

The drawbacks of a free teleseminar include:

- You won't make any money upfront.

- It can be difficult to get your guest speakers to mention your call to their list if they won't be making any upfront money from it.

- Sometimes, something offered for free is perceived as having a lower value than something that comes with a price tag.

If your main goal is revenue generation, you could charge a fee for attending your teleseminar. Then again, you could opt for having it both ways: You could offer free access to the initial call and then charge for access to the recording and/or a transcript of the call. This way, you maximize the number of people added to your list, but you'll also raise some revenue because you provide people with the opportunity to purchase products.

The benefits of hosting a paid teleseminar:

- You will make money with each additional person who signs up to attend.

- Your speakers will be more likely to promote the call if they can earn a commission, i.e., if they receive a percentage—typically 50%—of any sales generated through their affiliate link.

- Your teleseminar might be perceived as more valuable if people must pay to gain access.

The drawbacks of a paid teleseminar:

- The more you charge, the fewer attendees you are likely to have.

- Implementation is more complicated, as you will have to set up a way to take and process payments as well as process affiliate commissions in the event that you are offering an affiliate program.

If you are just starting out, you may want to go with a free teleseminar. That way, you can work out the kinks, figure out the technology, and focus on learning the ropes without the added stress of dozens of people expecting a top-notch, glitch-free experience. Furthermore, you can focus on the teleseminar and won't have to worry about how to set up your shopping cart. Then, once you have figured out how everything works, you can begin charging for your teleseminars. Give thought to what will work best for your situation and your business. Take a look at the pluses and minuses of each model and choose the one that feels right for you.

Scheduling Your Teleseminar

If you will be the speaker, you can choose the day and time that works best for your schedule. However, if you are interviewing someone else and want to host the call live, you will need to take your interviewee's schedule into consideration. You could also pre-record the interview at a mutually convenient time and then make it available as a replay. Whichever way you go, here are some things to keep in mind when selecting the date and time for your teleseminar:

- Allow yourself enough time to build an audience and set up your system, but not so much time that you lose momentum. When announcing the date for your teleseminar, or teleseminar series, two weeks in the future is ideal, but one week is workable. Any more than two weeks and you run the risk of losing momentum; any less and you may not be able to get as many attendees as you'd like.

- Realize that you will never make everyone happy. There simply is no one time that is ideal for everyone. Your best bet is to pick a time that should work for the majority of your target market.

- There are times that are "better" than others. For instance, if your market includes working professionals, they may have trouble attending a teleseminar in the middle of the work day. Instead, choose evening or weekend hours. Stay-at-home moms and home-based business owners, on the other hand, may have more time during the day, but they are probably busy in the evening and on weekends.

- Remember that if people cannot attend, they might still want to download your teleseminar later, so make sure to offer an option for getting the information later, either free or for a fee.

- Offering a download of the transcript and MP3 recording gives your teleseminar announcements a longer shelf life. You can continue to invite people by promising that even if they missed the call, they can still get the download.

- If you are not sure what time is best, you can always schedule two calls! Of course, if you are interviewing someone, you will want to replay the original teleseminar rather than ask him or her to participate twice on the same topic.

- More is not always better. A two-hour teleseminar is not inherently more valuable than a one-hour call. In fact, more people would rather attend a one-hour call that moves along quickly than a two-hour call that drags on and on. Value your audience's time. If you really have enough content to go for two hours or more, you may want to schedule two separate installments or prepare your audience for an exciting, "marathon" call.

- Choose a time when you are at your best. If you are not a morning person, do not schedule your teleseminar for the early morning hours. Instead, pick a time when you are "on." After all, you are the star of the show.

Now that you have scheduled a time, let's talk about one of the most important skills of a teleseminar host: Interviewing.

Online Interviews as a Source of Rich and Vibrant Content

One of the easiest and most effective ways to generate relevant and pertinent content is produce an audio interview series. By doing so, you will be providing valuable substance to your audience while building relationships with the people you interview. I have developed a deeper relationship with each person I have interviewed on my online radio show and teleseminar series (www.BookMarketingTeleseminars.com) and my listeners are really enjoying the content.

Interviews provide incredible content for a teleseminar series in your topic area. You can then sell those interviews individually or as part of a series. You can allow people to listen from your website or to be able to download the audio and transcripts. You can host an interview series on your interest topic and that could become valuable content for your members.

As far as whom to interview, that depends on who your audience is. As an example, my audience is nonfiction authors who want to learn more about marketing their books online. When I look for people to interview, I seek people who are experts in this area. This provides them with exposure to a new audience while providing my listeners with relevant and pertinent subject matter.

It could be that you already know people who speak on topics of interest to your audience. If not, you can visit LinkedIn groups, on your topic, and take note of who is posting articles and answering questions in a way that adds value to that community. Another place to locate relevant content and connect with potential speakers is at EzineArticles.com. Do a search on the topics you would like to interview people on, spend some time reviewing the articles, and visit the websites of the authors. Reach out to people who you feel can provide a real benefit to your audience. Providing an opportunity for speakers to gain exposure to new people in their target audience can create a win/win situation.

Having an expert take part in your teleseminar has a number of advantages:

- You do not have to rely on your own expertise; your guest will be there to educate your audience.

- You will achieve expert status by association. Think of Oprah. She isn't a weight loss expert, but because she has interviewed dozens of experts in that field, she is seen as a health and fitness guru in her own right.

- You can bring new expertise to your audience. Offering an added perspective to your audience raises your value in their eyes. You become a "connector," someone who knows all the right people.

- You can get in front of new prospects. Many experts have audiences or lists of their own; and, by your interviewing these people, you will inadvertently have the opportunity to get in front of their audience. This will provide you with exposure to new contacts and potential clients.

- You can do soft-sells on affiliate products. If you are an affiliate for a book on time management, for example, you can bring the author in front of your audience for a Q&A session. Then, when the author mentions her book, you provide your affiliate link and get a commission for every book your audience buys.

When selecting a guest expert there are several factors to consider before issuing them an invitation. First of all, decide if he is a good fit for your audience? Do not invite a hamburger chef when your audience consists of vegetarians and expect to get a warm response. Since the primary goal for having a guest expert is to bring value to your listeners, make sure that you select guest speakers who have something valuable to say. Make sure you are spending your time—and your audience's time—wisely by offering something unique, interesting, educational, and/or entertaining.

From a marketing standpoint, you may want to focus on guests who have a large following. This is not a must-have, but it definitely helps if your speaker has a large audience of her own and is willing to promote your teleseminar. It is an additional bonus if she has products or services to promote. If you are hoping to earn commissions by promoting her products or services, find out how her affiliate program works, and if her products or services are right for your audience.

When approaching potential guests, begin with people you have a relationship with or those you have familiarity with. Typically, you will be able to locate their contact information on their website. Write a polite, short email introducing yourself and why you think your market would be a good match for his or her area of expertise. Be sure to include the date(s) of your teleseminar and how long the interview will take. Then, let the prospective interviewee know what's in it for him or her. For example, there will be exposure to an enthusiastic new market or a share of the proceeds.

Create a page on your website where you can feature photographs and topics your guests will be speaking on. As your list of interviewees grows, you will have an impressive portfolio to share with potential future guests. People want to be associated with other successful people so this strategy will attract "big names" in your industry.

This is really not a complicated process. Choose someone you would like to hear from, write a polite note to invite him or her, and then move on if you do not hear back from this person or if he or she is not able to participate at this time. A "No" isn't a "No" forever; it is just a "No" for today, so keep in touch with people and, over time, they could end up being one of your guests.

Interviewing Tips

I am sure you have listened to poor interviewers—or interviewees—and that you have wondered how soon you could turn off the radio (or the TV) or hang up the phone. Then, there are the fabulous interviewers who are so skilled at pulling great information from their guests that you could listen for hours.

Here's how to make sure your own interview is top-notch:

1. Prepare. Good lawyers have a saying, "Don't ask a question you don't already know the answer to." While you don't need to predict every word out of your interviewees' mouths, you should have a strong idea of their areas of expertise, background, and value to your audience. If you are not familiar with them, investigate: Read up on them online, get a copy of their books, listen to other interviews they have done, and visit their websites. Basically, be sure you know who they are and what they can offer your listeners. It is a common practice to ask your guests to provide eight to ten questions that they would like to discuss during their interview. This is a win/win situation and removes the stress of wondering what you'll ask them.

2. Share. Share your plan for the teleseminar with your interviewee. Do you plan to guide the session with questions, or would you like your expert to take the floor? Do you want him to mention the product or service he has to offer, or do you want the teleseminar to be pitch-free? What are the main questions you will ask? Who is your audience? Pass this information on to your expert so he or she can prepare.

3. Listen. I have heard interviews where I got the impression that the interviewer was not even listening to the expert's answers. No matter what her guest said, she never really responded and simply read the next question off a sheet. Do not make that mistake. Listen and respond thoughtfully to your guest's answers, and ask the kinds of follow-up questions your audience might wish they could ask.

4. Interact. In keeping with the last point, ask a few deeper questions that are sparked by your guest's responses to questions asked. The best interviews are the ones where the questions go a little deeper than in most other interviews on the same topic. There is value in going beyond the information that has been covered time and time again. Be different by being more thoughtful and insightful. That does not mean you should ask rude, personal, or deeply confrontational questions. Just be curious, open, and really involved in the conversation. After all, this is a teleseminar, not a news report.

5. Disappear. One of the biggest mistakes you can make is putting yourself in the spotlight. As the interviewer, your job is to step into the background and let your expert take center stage. You have chosen this person because he has valuable information, so let him share it! Do not monopolize the microphone, keep turning the conversation back to yourself, or start every sentence with "I."

Good interviewing takes practice, but the good news is that you can start growing your skills right now! Practice on people you come in contact with: standing in line at the bank, over dinner with your family, or while watching the kids play on the playground. Ask people about themselves, and practice listening and responding. You might even learn something in the process!

Getting Publicity

If you do not have a built-in list of thousands, you will need to generate some publicity for your teleseminar if you want others outside of your immediate "world" to attend. Here are some ways you can start spreading the word:

- Email your list. Even if you only have a few dozen subscribers, let them know what you have planned. Encourage them to invite their own friends and contacts.

- Include a catchy tagline and link to your sign up page, in your email and forum signatures.

- Blog about it. Write a short overview about your guest expert or provide an introduction to the topic you will be covering. You could even invite readers to submit questions, which will increase their involvement in your teleseminar.

- Mention it on the various social media platforms where you have an active presence. Tweet about it and post updates on Facebook, LinkedIn, and other social media sites. Do not be afraid to mention it several times, and be sure to include a link to your sign-up page.

- Create a short, pre-interview audio or video and distribute it through sites such as YouTube, Viddler, Metacafe, or iTunes. Provide an overview of the topic, or share a sneak peek of what you will be covering. Of course, be sure to provide a link to your sign-up page.

- Post it on teleseminar announcement services, such as SeminarAnnouncer.com, ccuLearning.com, or SeeYouOnTheCall.com.

- Post an announcement in the events sections of Facebook, LinkedIn, and other social media communities you are a part of.

- Participate in groups on LinkedIn. One way to promote your teleseminars is by actively participating in groups on LinkedIn. Join a few groups that are of interest to your target audience, as well as a few that cater to people who serve your target audience. Once you join a group, introduce yourself and begin to contribute to the conversation. Take care not to step in and try to sell to the other members. You want to sell them on you, not on your stuff! Participate in discussions, answer questions or ask questions that people can answer. Then, over time, people are going to know you, they're going to probably like you and they're going to trust you because you've been around for a while. Subsequently, when you have a teleseminar, you can certainly mention it to the group.

- Ask your contacts to spread the news. Leverage your relationships with others in your community and ask them to publicize your teleseminar.

- Write a few articles and announce your teleseminar in your resource box. To avoid disappointment, make sure that the link leads to a page that will also offer access to the replay after the live event.

- Ask your guest to mention the call in his or her newsletter and to tweet or blog about it.

- Mention it in your own newsletter. Do not assume your list will put your teleseminar on their calendar the first time they hear about it. Remind them a few times, especially on the day of the actual event!

- Don't forget in-person promotions. If your teleseminar is related to parenting, tell your friends and fellow parents at your kids' schools. Also, why not ask your PTA if you can mention it in their newsletter? If your topic is personal finance, local accountants may be willing to mention it to their clients. They are often looking for valuable information to offer to their mailing lists. Think outside the box—and off the computer!

- Sell your book as the "ticket" to your teleseminar. Another way to grow your list and sell more books is by having the "ticket" to your live teleseminar be the receipt to your purchased book. You can create a special page on your blog where people are invited to purchase your book and either email you a copy of their receipt or enter their receipt number into the provided field on your opt-in form. By doing so, they will receive an email invitation to an upcoming live teleseminar where you will be speaking on the topic of your book. You can also program your opt-in form to take people to a thank-you page on your site where they will find details of the upcoming teleseminar.

There are literally hundreds of ways you can promote your teleseminar. The more time you spend, the more buzz you can create. If you have limited time, just focus on a few, key strategies and begin promoting.

Monetize Your Teleseminars

Why do people offer teleseminars? Some of them want to get the word out about their causes, but most hosts know that teleseminars are a great way to make money—and some of them make a very nice living with their teleseminars.

That brings us to what you can do to monetize your teleseminars, thus earning income from repurposing your teleseminar recording and transcript into a wide variety of products. Let's explore what you can do with this material to bring value to your audience and brand yourself as an expert in your field.

The word "repurposing" is a term that is becoming known in Internet marketing circles. An example of repurposing would be, as in the above example, providing an MP3 recording of your call. Another example would be for you to provide the transcript of your call. In essence you are taking your content and turning it, repurposing it, into different formats.

Taking this concept a step further, what if you were to take your transcripts and break them into smaller chunks, which can either become the foundation for an eBook, manual, or workbook, or can be used as part of your weekly email training? There are many ways that you can repurpose material in order to brand yourself and offer more value to your audience.

One easy way to monetize your teleseminar is to offer an "upsell" once someone registers to attend the free live event. In addition to being able to listen to the recorded call online, offer the attendee the ability to purchase the MP3 download and the transcript.

You can also monetize your events by promoting, endorsing, or reviewing related products that offer you an affiliate commission in exchange for people purchasing products through your affiliate link. Word of mouth advertising is the most powerful form and there are many companies, who offer products that would benefit your audience. These companies would be delighted to send you money for promoting them to your audience.

You can promote products, in the form of recommendations, during your teleseminar. You can write review articles about products you would like to promote. You can also post banner images, embedded with your affiliate link, on your blog or website.

Following are two ways that you can make money with your teleseminar:

- **Charge for registration.** Charge people for access to your teleseminar. How much you can charge ranges from a few dollars to thousands of dollars. Obviously, the higher the rate, the higher the value and perceived value needs to be. I suggest that you keep the registration fees on the lower end of the scale when you first get started. It will give you a chance to prove your value to your market before you ask them to invest huge amounts of cash up front.

- **Sell your own products.** You can also sell your own products either towards the end of the teleseminar or even after the call, in a follow-up email. Make sure those products are related to the call, and that they are useful and targeted to your market.

- **Bundle your calls together.** Think creatively about new ways to package and present your content. Take a series of related teleseminar calls and bundle the audios together into a larger product for sale to your market.

- **Turn your calls into physical products.** Of course, you can also turn your calls into physical products. The audios will make fine CD sets and the transcriptions can be turned into physical books. Then again, you could also put the transcripts into binders—maybe along with action sheets—and command a much higher price by selling your combined set as a home study course. Kunaki (www.Kunaki.com) and Vervante (www.Vervante.com) are two companies that can turn your digital content into physical products. They both offer on-demand publishing and order fulfillment.

As you can see, there is plenty of money to be made, even if you do not charge an upfront fee for your teleseminar registration—and the best thing is this: You can use several of the above methods and turn your calls into multiple streams of income.

Technology

Just a few short years ago, teleseminars would have been impossible to do or prohibitively expensive. However, now, they are inexpensive and even free, depending on which service you use. In addition, you will need a few extra tools to reach and connect with your market, especially if you plan to turn your teleseminars into multiple streams of income. Here's a rundown of the key tools to add to your arsenal:

- **A way to capture your leads:** The first thing you need is something called a "squeeze page," or an "opt-in page," which is a one-page website that invites visitors to provide their name and email address in exchange for access to your teleseminar. You need this squeeze page, as it will allow you to build your list, which you can then use to send information to your subscribers, including information about any upcoming teleseminars.

  You can either set up a separate page or website or make the opt-in form part of an existing page, such as on the sidebar of your blog. Either way, you will need a place for people to go to subscribe to your list. This brings us to the next thing you'll need: an email management system.

- **An email list management system:** An email management system, usually referred to as an auto-responder system, is an indispensable part of your online business. While there are various options available, you'd be wise to pick a reputable third-party auto-responder service, such as Aweber (www.WebmailConnections.com) or 1ShoppingCart (www.BestShoppingCartSystem). These services ensure great deliverability of your emails and will also insulate you from spam complaints, which could otherwise have a detrimental impact on your budding business.

  Any of these auto-responder services will allow you to create lists and send email to your subscribers. You can send them your teleseminar information, as well as follow up with additional information after the call and, of course, you can invite them to your next calls.

An auto-responder gives you several options: 1) You can set up a sequence of emails that will be sent out in pre-determined intervals after someone first opts into your system, or 2) You can broadcast messages to all your subscribers (or all members of certain lists) at once, or 3) You can even schedule broadcasts ahead of time.

- **A payment processor:** If you plan to make money with your teleseminars, you will need a way to take payments. There are a number of options, from PayPal (www.PayPal.com) to ClickBank (www.ClickBank.com) to a shopping cart system like 1ShoppingCart (www.BestShoppingCartSystem.com). Selecting the best option depends on whether or not you are planning to offer affiliate commissions and what other products you want to sell.

  If you plan on building a business around your teleseminars, you should seriously consider integrating an affiliate program into your system. You can do this with 1ShoppingCart, which also offers an auto-responder service, or you can integrate a third-party affiliate program, such as ClickBank (www.ClickBank.com) or ShareaSale (www.ShareaSale.com), into your program, along with AWeber as your auto-responder service and PayPal as your shopping cart.

- **A teleseminar service:** Obviously, you will also need a teleseminar service. There are many free teleseminar services, such as FreeConferenceCalling (www.FreeConferenceCalling.com) and

BlogTalkRadio (www.BlogTalkRadio.com). There are also paid services available, including the one that is the most popular among Internet marketers: Instant Teleseminar (www.WebTeleseminars.com). They offer a three-week trial for a dollar and have an excellent customer service department. In the following section we will discuss these services.

Options for the Recording and Delivery of Your Teleseminars

Free Conference Calling

My favorite free option is Free Conference Calling (www.FreeConferenceCalling.com). I recommend this service because they are reliable and have a Web application that allows you to see the names and phone numbers of your attendees. Your attendees also have the ability to punch in a code to indicate that they have, or are responding to a question you are asking.

Your call recordings are hosted on the Free Conference Calling site and you can even post a link to allow your audience to access either single recordings or all of the recordings in a series. They give you the ability to download the recording to your computer. I recommend that you download each call and save it to your hard drive. While your account is open, you can link straight to your call archives area; but, if you ever cancel your account, all of your recordings will be on that system, and they would be lost. Therefore, download copies of the recordings just to be safe.

BlogTalkRadio

Another way to get your message out across the Internet is to set up an online radio show on BlogTalkRadio (www.BlogTalkRadio.com). This is a free platform that gets a lot of traffic. This is also a fun way to build your name brand recognition and become known as an expert on your topic. Once you've recorded your first show, you can download a widget to place on your blog or website. This will make your content readily available to your community.

When you set up your account, be sure to strategically pick your user name, as that is going to be your station name and what people type in as part of the Web address. Select something that reflects your business or the topic on which you will be speaking. BlogTalkRadio has an option that allows you to easily and automatically send the replay of your broadcast over to iTunes.

While BlogTalkRadio is a fantastic platform, it may not be best for every situation. If you broadcast on BlogTalkRadio, your content is free and available to anyone and everyone. If you want to maintain the proprietary rights to your content, then you won't want to publish the whole program on BlogTalkRadio. You can use BlogTalkRadio to leverage a preview show. In this way, you get the benefit of lots of exposure and the ability to invite people to your site to learn more about you and your programs. I would only use this method on occasion, as you will want to give substantial content to your listeners so that they come back and tell others about your show.

You can also use BlogTalkRadio as a platform from which to share a weekly or monthly interview series, where experts speak on a wide variety of topics, related to your primary area of focus. At the beginning and end of each call you can mention your teleseminar series, which focuses on a *specific* topic, and invite your listeners to register to attend your event.

Webcast Platform and Telephone Interface with Instant Teleseminar

The most popular, premium, teleseminar service is Instant Teleseminar (www.WebTeleseminars.com). In addition to being able to record and rebroadcast your recording, you can see the call-in details of each of your attendees, conduct polls, offer a webcast option to your listeners, show PowerPoint presentations, and have an instant website where people can go to listen in live or access the replay afterwards.

The webcast option is great if your listeners are across the globe and for those who do not want to tie up their phone lines. It also provides the ability to reach a much larger audience because you are not limited by the number of callers on the phone lines. They offer a 21-day trial to test out the service and hold a few teleseminars in order to experience firsthand all they have to offer. You can cancel your trial or your subscription at any point just by sending an email to their support staff and they have excellent customer support.

You can use the service to reach listeners anywhere in the world. They can call into your teleseminar phone number or they can listen to the webcast via the Internet. The webcast option is quite popular because it offers the listener more flexibility. The downside of the webcast option is when the speaker opens up the call and asks for questions. Those on the webcast will not be heard. However, they do have the ability to submit their questions via a text box on the webcast page. This service can expand your audience because you can have an unlimited number who can access the webcast.

The webcast page actually looks like a custom-designed Web page which you can customize from a wide selection of colorful options. Your listeners go there to get the call details, such as the time, date, and phone number, as well as access to the online audio. The ability to add Web links and a big button to your webcast page is another great feature. You can offer people the action guide for your teleseminar or a free downloadable report, as well as access to your blog, social networks, or your website. You should test any services you are considering to make sure they meet your needs. Don't forget to give them a trial run, so you can see how user-friendly they are, *before* you schedule your teleseminar.

With any of these options, you can create and run a fully-automated teleseminar with a minimal outlay of upfront cash. Just remember that while there are certainly a number of free options, occasionally it is a good idea to invest a little bit to get a more robust, scalable, and dependable service. It may also provide you with a much more professional presence.

Ready to Get Started

As you can see, hosting and producing your own teleseminar is very manageable and easy to do. Start off by creating a practice teleseminar where a friend or colleague interviews you. This will give you a chance to get familiar with the features of your service and download the audio recording. You may even want to have someone interview you on a topic in which you have expertise. You can then have the audio transcribed for future blog posts and to work out any of the kinks with your transcription company.

Teleseminars are as simple as conducting a group conference call, but with many extra benefits. You can use teleseminars to increase your market reach, establish yourself as an expert, bond with your audience, and earn serious money. While there are a lot of moving parts to keep track of, don't get so caught up in the details and thus lose sight of the big picture. The most important thing to keep in mind is your primary goal, which is to provide valuable information to your audience.

My hopes are that you now have a roadmap for planning and implementing your own teleseminars. Begin by holding your first teleseminar with a few trusted friends, record your event, have it transcribed, rinse and repeat. One of the most powerful ways to create content is to prepare a list of prioritized interview questions on your topic. Have a trusted colleague—ideally someone with an attractive "radio voice"—ask you each of these questions. Answer in as much detail as possible in a positive and upbeat voice. You will then have the audio track for your first product as well as a recording which can be transcribed and turned into anything from a blog post to your next book!

In the next chapter we will be discussing ways you can repurpose your teleseminar recordings into a wide variety of products. By delivering the message of your book in multiple formats, you will be able to reach more people, sell more books and grow your audience.

Teleseminars can open up incredible opportunities in your business and help you sell more books. When you stay focused on your goals and follow the steps presented in this chapter, your teleseminar will be a success, and you will effectively grow your business and your brand. Here's to a long and happy series of teleseminars, for both you and your audience!

Keys to
Teleseminar Success

- Team up with a friend or colleague to host and record an interview style teleseminar. Choose someone with a nice speaking voice as you will be able to share the audio recording of this interview.

- Compose a list of 8-12 questions about you, your book and why you wrote your book. This will provide you with a great audio recording as well as great written content once you have the audio transcribed.

- Set up your teleseminar service and schedule your call. Invite a few close friends to attend.

- On the day of the call mute the line so only you and the person interviewing you are heard. This will make for a clean recording. Conduct the interview, making sure to record it.

- Have the audio transcribed so that you can repurpose the content. As an example, you can create an eBook to offer as a gift to your opt-in subscribers.

Teleseminar Resources

1ShoppingCart:	www.BestShoppingCartSystem
AnyMeeting:	www.AnyMeeting.com
Aweber:	www.WebmailConnections.com
BlogTalkRadio:	www.BlogTalkRadio.com
ClickBank:	www.ClickBank.com
Easy Video Player:	www.TryEasyVideoPlayer.com
FreeConferenceCalling:	
	www.FreeConferenceCalling.com
Instant Teleseminar:	www.WebTeleseminars.com
Kunaki:	www.Kunaki.com
PayPal:	www.PayPal.com
Vervante:	www.Vervante.com
Wishlist:	www.WishlistMembershipPlugin.com
YouSendIt:	www.YouSendIt.com

Chapter Five:
Information Marketing for Multiple Paydays

Your book is the doorway to developing multiple streams of income. From a digital eBook to a high-priced coaching program, your book provides you with the content and credibility to offer your audience more while increasing your streams of income.

Information products are fantastic tools to increase profits, credibility, traffic and much more. The term "information product" can apply to all factual books, reports transcripts, audio recordings and video recordings. In the online world, the phrase is generally used to describe electronically-deliverable, knowledge-based products. They are often known as digital goods and are available to download or are emailed to the customer.

You can generate a passive income on the Internet when you create a single product and repurpose it into multiple products, thus getting paid several times on the same content. Some people prefer to read while others like to listen to a CD in their car and still others prefer to view a video. Why not provide all of these options and give people a variety of products to choose from?

From eBooks to videos, there are a wide variety of products that can easily be produced from your teleseminar recordings and transcripts. Offering a wide range of options not only provides additional revenue sources for you, it also makes your message more accessible and easier for more people to digest.

Here is a spectrum of ideas to choose from:

- Transcripts
- eBooks
- Reports
- MP3 Recordings
- CD Recordings
- eCourses
- Workbooks
- Blog Posts
- Ezines
- Newsletters
- Home Study Courses
- Coaching Programs
- PowerPoint Video Presentations

Transcripts

Offer your teleseminar transcript as a part of your package or as an upsell for a higher price. You can easily offer this by using a service such as Verbal Ink (www.VerbalInk.com). They will transcribe the recording and turn it into a Microsoft Word file for you. When selecting a transcription service, it is recommended to select one that employs native English speaking transcriptionists. This will save you editing time and prevent embarrassment. Your transcripts are a direct reflection upon you and the quality of your work.

eBooks and Reports

You can easily turn your teleseminar transcript into an eBook or special report. The basic difference between an eBook and a special report is the number of pages.

Simply add a footer with your name and website along with a title page, table of contents, author page, and a resource page, and you are good to go.

MP3 Recordings

Your audio recordings are an excellent way to market your brand, service, and/or product. You can host your recordings on your blog or website with services such as Audio Acrobat (www.AudioAcrobat.com), BlogTalkRadio (www.BlogTalkRadio.com), or Easy Video Player (www.TryEasyVideoPlayer.com).

CD Recordings

Once you have your digital MP3 recording, you can then turn it into a CD that can be mailed to your customers. Kunaki (www.Kunaki.com) and Vervante (www.Vervante.com) are two companies that offer print-on-demand and drop shipping services.

eCourse

You can create an eCourse, and deliver it via email. Your auto-responder service allows you to program the delivery sequence and frequency of your eCourse modules. You may want the content to be delivered every day or once a week for a specific period of time.

Workbooks

Use content from your course to create questions for people to think about and respond to. Workbooks can include key points, essential information, and fill-in-the-blank lines. They also provide space for people to take notes on what they are learning. A workbook adds value to your course as it encourages participation and increases the likelihood that people will take action.

Blog Posts

Another great source of content is right on your blog. Taking your previous blog posts and turning them into an eBook, special report, eCourse, articles or content for your eZine is a quick and easy way to produce an information product.

eZines and Newsletters

An eZine is an online magazine or newsletter. It can be sent out weekly or monthly, via email. It can be in plain text and easy to read even on a cell phone, or it can be pretty and colorful, with images and in your branded colors. A newsletter is much like an eZine but is a publication that is sent through the postal mail. Your repurposed content provides you with useful articles for your eZines and your newsletters.

Home Study Courses

Information that you have created in audio, video, or written form can all be repurposed into a home study course. You can offer a "green" version of downloadable digital products or a "big box" version that you ship to customers through the mail. Digital home study courses are very popular as your customers can download the content to their computer.

Physical products add a lot of value to your program, however creating these products and putting a delivery system in place is more costly and a bit more involved than creating a downloadable digital program, which can be delivered via email. There are print-on-demand services however, such as Kunaki (www.Kunaki.com) and Vervante (www.Vervante.com), which will streamline this process for you. They offer everything from design layout to shipping your products to your customers.

Develop a Coaching Program

An alternative to a home-study course is to create a coaching program. You can offer individual and group coaching at a variety of levels. You may consider offering email, telephone, or forum support to your members. You can also offer group or individual training via conference calls or online webinars, as part of your coaching program. By offering a coaching program you are investing in your future, as this is a fantastic way to build strong relationships with your clients.

PowerPoint Video Presentations

You can create a PowerPoint presentation, and use screen capture software such as Camtasia (www.CamtasiaStudio.com) or Jing Project (www.JingProject.com) to produce a video. You can even use your Webcam to make a smaller box inside your PowerPoint with you talking about the presentation. They call this feature a "picture-in-picture". We will discuss these formats in more depth in Chapter Seven.

You are not limited by geography when selling online. The whole world can consume your products because you have put them out there on the Internet. Have fun, be creative and enjoy creating several streams of income from the same content.

Grow Your Business with Information Products

There are two main uses for information products: selling them or giving them away. The reason for doing the first is obvious; you receive a fixed amount of money for each product you sell. However, the reasons for giving away your information product might seem less clear; after all, why would you spend time creating a quality product if you are not going to make any money on it?

Here are a few of the reasons you might consider giving away an information product:

- To exchange it for a name and email address for your list

- As an incentive to subscribe to your membership site

- Because it includes affiliate links that will make you money in the long term

- To increase your reputation as a subject-matter expert

- To build up credibility with your customers, so they will buy a higher value product

Creating your own information products can provide you with a profitable source of income as well as build up your reputation as an expert in your subject area. Before you start to create your information product, there are some criteria it needs to fulfill. Ensuring that your product meets the following standards may save you a great deal of frustration and disappointment when it comes time for you to sell it.

Information Product Criteria Checklist

✓ **Is your product exceptional?** Selling an inferior product may make you money in the short term, but it will damage your online reputation and lose you customers in the long run. Generally, when a customer buys from you once, she is more likely to do so again. However, if a customer is not happy with the quality of your product, it is likely that she will never buy from you again and that she will discourage her network from doing so.

✓ **Do people want it? Is there enough demand?** You can have a superb, quality product; but, if there is no demand, you won't make any sales. On the other hand, if you can create a product that people really need, your sales effort will be much easier.

✓ **Does it look like a professional product?** Presentation is at least as important as content in establishing the credibility of your product, if not more so. A great logo, clear graphics, and a professional, high-impact front cover will all help to increase your sales and gain the loyalty of your customers.

Convert Your Content into a Different Medium

Here's an idea that you can use alone or in combination with other content repurposing ideas. For example, you may:

- Turn a text product into an audio product.
- Transcribe an audio product into a text product.
- Turn an article into a video.
- Turn a video into an audio.
- Create every other combination of changing a text, audio or video product into a different format.

The reasons for doing this are simple:

1. First, doing so accommodates people with disabilities. For example, transcribing an audio helps your customers who are hearing-impaired.

2. Changing the medium also means you can accommodate those with different learning styles and preferences. Some people have a hard time remembering what they've read, but they love watching videos. Others may have just the opposite need or preference.

Changing the format often means you change the perceived value of the product, which allows you to charge more. Generally, audio has a higher perceived value than text-only content, and videos are judged to be more valuable than text and audio. Consequently, if you turn a written book into a video series, you can usually charge much more for it.

How to Make Residual Income from Your Information Products

Creating an eBook or similar information product is a great way to make an ongoing income, as once you have finished it, you can keep marketing and selling it over and over again to different audiences. You can also provide follow up material and updated versions of your information product.

Your income from an individual sale does not have to stop at the initial sale, however. There are many ways to develop income streams from your information products.

To begin with, you can use your information product to market other products. These can be digital products, physical products, or a subscription to a service such as a membership site. Pre-sell your products within the text of your information product and then provide a link to the sales page for that product.

Give Away Samples

Do you ever go to the super market and nibble on a free sample only to grab the product and drop it in your cart. This is called impulse shopping. Giving away free excerpts from your information products in exchange for your customer's email address can be an effective sales technique. You can offer these excerpts as short articles, audios, or videos. Once you have your customer's contact information, you can follow up by email, offering them the rest of the product at a special rate. Make sure the extracts that you choose to give away are some of the best parts of the product, but that they leave your customers with the feeling of wanting to know more.

Network

Joining various discussion forums related to the topic of your books, and thus your products, is a great way to generate additional sales. If you post relevant and well-informed comments, you will quickly be seen as an expert in that field and people will be interested to see what else you have to say, on your blog or in your books, eBooks, or reports.

Don't be in too much of a hurry to get the sale. It is essential to lay the groundwork and build up a relationship with other members of the discussion forum before you mention your book or programs.

Most discussion forums allow you to put a link back to your site at the bottom of your post, so make sure your link points to a page that best illustrates who you are and what you have to offer.

Launch a Membership Site

Another use for your subject matter is as content for a membership site. A membership site provides your members with a central location for accessing their content and serves as an online "community center", if you will. Your membership site also provides you with ongoing passive income.

A simple yet powerful system for creating your membership site is to install a membership plugin, such as Wishlist Membership Plugin (www.WishlistMembershipPlugin.com) on your WordPress blog. This program allows you to easily turn your blog into a highly functioning membership site. You can charge a fixed rate or you can charge customers a monthly access fee. You can also choose whether to have all of the content available from day one, or whether you'd prefer to have new content added weekly, for example.

Membership sites can be extremely popular and profitable, as you can earn a monthly, residual (passive) income. The problem with monthly membership sites is that you continuously need to be creating new content and updating your site on an ongoing basis.

The solution is to create a membership site with a fixed duration. Instead of members' paying a monthly fee indefinitely, you can set up your membership site in such a way that people sign up and pay either a fixed rate for the entire program or a monthly fee for a pre-determined amount of time, such as three months, six months, or one year. You set the duration based on how many modules you would like to deliver.

Your membership site can offer a general members' area where members have access to new content each week for the number of weeks you've promised them. You can program your auto-responder to deliver a weekly notification inviting your members to access new content in the members' area.

You only need to program your membership site and auto-responder once. You just "set it and forget it." The exact content any one member is receiving during a specific week is dependent on where he or she is in the auto-responder series. This is simple, easy and a very profitable way to reuse your content!

Turn Your Content into a Lead-Generating Presentation

Whether you have text, audio, or video products, you can easily turn this content into a live presentation. Then you can give this live presentation via a teleseminar, webinar, or even as an in-person speaking engagement. Your goal is to build a list of prospects by having people register for your free presentation. Then at the end of your talk, you can encourage people to buy your book and other products and/or register for your paid workshop.

Turn Your Content into a Paid Presentation

You can turn your text, audio, or even video content into a presentation. However, instead of offering the presentation or workshop for free as a lead generator, you offer it as a paid program.

These two ideas work well together. You can repurpose your content to create a free, lead-generating workshop or other presentation. Then you can invite your participants to enjoy the next level of training by registering for your paid workshop.

Deliver Your Content in a New Format

Earlier, we discussed how audio products have a higher perceived value than text products, and videos have a higher perceived value than both text and audio products. Here, the idea is to turn a digital product into a physical product. Turning digital products into physical products usually boosts the perceived value of the product. That means you can generally charge more for your shipped DVD versus the downloadable video you offer on your website.

For example:

- You can turn your eBook into a paperback book by going to a book printer or using a print-on-demand company such as CreateSpace.com.

- You can turn your downloadable and streaming videos into physical DVDs that you ship.

- You can create physical CDs from your audio recordings.

Of course, you can do the inverse by turning your physical products into downloadable digital products.

Turning physical products into digital products solves the need for instant gratification, which is particularly important when you are serving an audience that has an immediate need for your product or services. For example, if you are selling a product about "how to soothe a sunburn," people are not going to want to wait for the product to arrive on their doorstep. They want and need the solution now, which is why they will be looking for downloadable information.

Advantages of Creating Information Products

The idea of putting together an information product from scratch may seem daunting, but take it step by step and it can be a very simple process. Creating your own information products can grow your business in many ways. You can give your product away to grow your list or provide your product as a bonus or an incentive to people when they purchase one of your other products.

One of the main advantages of creating your own information products is that they will add credibility to your business and enable you to build up a reputation as an expert in your subject area. Having successful information products in your portfolio will enable you to successfully launch additional products and programs.

In the following chapter you will discover another powerful use for your content. This strategy will increase your books sales and your reach.

Keys to
Information Marketing Success

- Repurpose the transcript from one of your teleseminar recordings into three different formats.

- Consider creating a PowerPoint presentation that you can turn into a video.

- Read through the transcript and pull out several key points. Repurpose this content into several blog posts. Post these to your site.

- Identify blogs that attract your target audience. Contact the site owners to determine if they would be interested in having you post as a guest blogger. Pull content from your transcript and publish an article on their site. Make sure to add your name and book title along with a link back to your site.

- Upload your audio interview to your blog and send out a *tweet* to Twitter and *update* on Facebook, inviting people to listen in.

Information Marketing Resources

Animoto Video: www.Animoto.com

Audio Acrobat: www.AudioAcrobat.com

AWeber: www.WebmailConnections.com

CamStudio: www.Camstudio.org

Camtasia: www.techsmith.com/camtasia.asp

Easy Video Player: www.TryEasyVideoPlayer.com

Ezine Articles: www.EzineArticles.com

FreeConfernceCalling: www.FreeConferenceCalling.com

Instant Teleseminar: www.WebTeleseminars.com

Jing Project: www.JingProject.com

Kunaki: www.Kunaki.com

Verbal Ink: www.VerbalInk.com

Vervante: www.Vervante.com

Wishlist: www.WishlistMembershipPlugin.com

Chapter Six:
Reach New Audiences with Article Marketing

Article marketing is the process of creating short articles for publication and distribution by other websites and off-line publishers in exchange for at least one quality link back to your website or blog. Your teleseminar transcripts and information products provide you with a wealth of information to draw from when composing articles.

Article marketing can be one of the most effective, free methods for getting targeted traffic to your website and thus more exposure for your book. Articles can be posted to article directories, which are websites made up entirely of articles submitted by authors. Publishing an article to an article directory is usually free.

Article directories provide a central location for people to access your articles. One of the benefits of posting your articles to an article directory is that blog owners and newsletter publishers can use articles from article directories in order to provide more content for their readers. As long as they leave your bio box and live links intact, they are permitted to publish your articles.

Articles can be used for many purposes, with the primary goals of highlighting you as an expert in your field, gaining increased search-engine rankings, and having your articles shared by people with large followings. Articles can be submitted to article directories, where others can access your content via the article directory search engine. In essence, article directories are repositories which allow people to publish articles from the directory to their blog, newsletter, and Ezine as long as they leave the live links (meaning when someone clicks on your link, it will take them to the site you've listed) and that they include your resource box. The goal of article marketing is not only to get your articles listed in the article directories, but to get your articles published on blogs and in Ezines and newsletters, gaining you exposure to new audiences.

While it may seem counter-intuitive to provide your content for free to other websites, there are many advantages. Following are several benefits of article marketing:

- **Link Love.** When your content is published on blogs and in eZines, you receive a link back to your blog. When properly optimized, this link will assist in helping you rate more highly for search engine results. When you rank more highly in Google and other search engines, you'll get more organic traffic to your blog and more traffic means more readers!

- **Validation.** When your articles are published by others, you receive an unofficial recommendation from the publisher. It's as if you are getting a stamp of approval from another blogger or website owner. This recommendation will further your reputation and drive more readers to your site.

- **Expert Status.** When you can say that you have published numerous articles on your given topic, you increase your Web presence and ability to claim expert status. That means your trust level increases and you have more credibility.

There are a number of low-cost or no-cost online article directories where you can share your articles. This makes article marketing a cost-effective way to publicize your website and, thus, to gain more exposure for your book.

There are four key components to successful article marketing:

1. Target keywords
2. Well-written titles
3. Good content
4. An enticing resource box

In order for your article marketing to be as successful as possible, all four elements should be working in conjunction with one another. You must make sure to choose good keywords, craft interesting titles that encourage people to click through to read the article, write quality content, and create a resource box that makes people want to click. Your resource box usually contains a short bio along with a link to your blog or website and is placed directly under the article.

A great way to lead more readers to your resource box is to place a statement such as the following one prior to the resource box, "Follow the link below to read more on this topic."

Article marketing is an easy and inexpensive way to increase your Web traffic and readership. Even if you have never written anything other than a blog post, you can leverage article marketing to make your blog readership skyrocket.

Gain More Exposure

Invite Your Readers to Reprint Your Content

A fantastic way to get in front of new audiences is to provide articles on your blog and invite others to share your content. This is a common practice and a wonderful way to provide readers with great content and access to your knowledge. On the page where you have your articles listed, you can post a statement, giving permission for others to reprint your articles as long as they include the author information you have listed at the end of each article. In that section, you can include your name and website, as well as an invitation, for example, for people to receive more tips by opting in to receive a special report.

Create a Facebook Fan Page for Your Articles

When setting up your fan page, you can pull in the RSS feed from your article directory accounts as well as from your blogs. An excerpt of your articles will then be displayed on your fan page. This will provide you with exposure to more readers and, again, position you as an authority on your subject.

Become a Guest Blogger on Sites Where Your Target Audience Frequents

Share your articles on other blogs, where you are featured as a guest blogger. This is an excellent way to get in front of new audiences and increase the likelihood of your articles being read. When other blog owners share your work, they are, in essence, endorsing you as an expert in your field. They have the trust of their readership, and if they are inviting their readers to read your articles as guest blog posts, then they are giving you their endorsement. To maximize your effectiveness, become a guest blogger on sites that attract your target audience and/or the people who serve your target audience.

Find Niche Article Directories and Publish Your Articles There

In addition to article directories that welcome articles on any topic under the sun, there are also niche directories which publish articles on specific topics or written by specific types of experts. To locate niche article directories, do a search in Google (www.Google.com) for terms such as, "niche article directories" or use the term for your niche topic. An example would be "book marketing article directories."

What to Write About

If you are an author wishing to increase your readership, article marketing can send highly targeted traffic your way. Everyone wants free traffic, but in order to get it through article marketing, you need to write articles. What do you write about?

You want to write about your topic area, your expertise and topics of interest to your target audience. By identifying problems and pains and providing solutions, you will quickly develop your readership.

Writing articles for article marketing is very similar to writing posts for your blog. Most experts recommend articles between 400-500 words, about the length of an average blog post. There are other similarities, too. When picking topics for articles, you want to:

- **Choose topics that are of interest to your target market.** If your blog audience is interior designers, your articles should be aimed at providing ideas and solutions to that same audience. Remember, your goal is to drive *targeted* traffic to your site. In other words, you want to attract people who will read your article, find something of interest, and click through to your blog for more of the same. Do not disappoint them by writing articles about one topic only to greet them at your blog with totally unrelated content. Readers will become annoyed and they will click away as fast as possible.

- **You want to develop a loyal and thirsty readership.** If you provide quality articles, people will be eager to read more of your work and find out more about you and your book. Through your articles, you will be able to connect with your readers, intrigue them with your message, have them click on the links in your resource box, and bring them to your website.

Write Keyword-Rich Articles

Keywords are the words people type into the article directory search engine when looking for articles on a specific topic. Keywords can be single words, separated by commas, as well as keyword phrases, which represent a phrase someone would type into a search engine such as Google. For example, if you were wanting to find out how to make vanilla ice cream, rather than typing the word "ice cream" into Google, you would most likely type in "how to make vanilla ice cream." This series of words is called a keyword phrase. You can seed your articles with both keywords and keyword phrases so that people can more easily locate your articles. Once you have identified your keywords and keyword phrases, you want to include them in your title as well as in the body of your article.

Eye-Catching Title

A good, keyword-rich title is critical, as that is the first thing readers will see when sifting through a list of articles. An effective title can make the difference between 20 people reading your article and 200 people reading it.

Here are some examples of types of titles that can attract readers:

- Ask a question
- List a benefit
- List ways to .....
- Use the word "Why"
- Use numbers in your titles

Write Articles on Topics That You Know Something About

Because you are positioning yourself as an expert, you should write on topics you feel comfortable with or do the research necessary to write an informative article on those topics.

It is important to remember that you are not writing a college dissertation. You are writing articles for real people searching for real solutions to real problems. People are looking for good quality content that is easy to skim, easy to read and that gets them the answer they are looking for in the least amount of time. Always keep that at the front of your mind when you set out to write your articles.

If you are passionate and knowledgeable about your subject area, most likely, you already have some ideas for articles. Begin collecting these ideas and keep this list in a notebook or saved in a file on your computer. This list will provide you with easy access to article ideas and can even provide you with the beginning of an outline for a series of articles.

Structuring Your Articles

While many article directories require a minimum of 400 words, writing a 500-word article will provide more information to your reader and will give you more of an opportunity to build a relationship with them. There are some simple ways to structure your article. A good, general rule when writing an article is to:

- Identify a pain or problem.

- Provide a solution.

- Create a natural flow from your article to the resource box.

- Invite your reader to access more on this topic by clicking on your resource box link.

End With a Compelling Resource Box

The resource box of your article can provide a smooth transition from one website to another. In addition to your articles being displayed on the article directories, they can also be shared on other websites. One of the requirements to be able to share articles from article directories is that the person sharing your article leaves your live links and resource box in place. By writing an article that is highly targeted to your market, you can lead readers from your article through to a well-crafted resource box that encourages them to click on a link, which will take them right to your website, where more information is waiting for them.

Now that you have successfully steered your reader to the bottom of the article by providing compelling content, you must *ask for the click*. Yes, I do mean explicitly instructing them to click on your link. This is what your resource box is for.

While it might seem natural to use your resource box to list all the great things about you, the truth is, by doing this, you are in essence saying to your reader, "The article is over; you can leave now." While readers are interested in your content and want to know your name and book title, in most cases, they are not going to take the time to study a long list of your credentials. The reader wants information and wants to know how he or she can solve his or her immediate problem. Therefore, the best resource boxes will tell the reader exactly what he needs to do to accomplish this. If you have done the job properly in your article, then you simply need to tell the reader that to solve his problem he only needs to "click here."

It is a good idea to include a benefit that the reader will be able to enjoy or to let him know what he might miss out on if he doesn't click. Don't fabricate information or get too "salesy" or you could lose that person as a potential customer.

Your ultimate goal in publishing articles is to capture the readers' attention, lead them through the article, and pull them to your blog or website.

Tips That Will Help Get Your Article Read

Be Informative

Writing an informative article is paramount to gaining your reader's trust; and, without trust, you have little hope of turning your reader into a customer.

Leave Them Wanting More

While you want your article to be informative, you do not want to give away all of your secrets. Leave your readers with a hint that there is more information they need so that they will keep reading to the bottom of your article and then click the link in your resource box.

For example, you might write a short article telling your readers how they can get rid of a common headache by mixing an onion with baking soda. Then, at the end of the article, you might say something like "However, you have to mix them in the correct amounts or you won't get the desired results!"

Next, tell them that they can find out what the right proportions are in an article on your blog. While they are there, you can also encourage them to receive a free report or purchase your book which will provide them with other natural, health secrets, for example.

You want to be informative, but to leave them wanting just one more piece of information that they can get by clicking the link in your resource box.

Format Your Article So That It Is Easy on the Eye

Write compelling content that causes the reader to want to keep reading by:

- Using white space between paragraphs,

- Adding bullet points to stress key points and make the information more accessible,

- Using bold headings and subheadings, and

- Using your keyword phrases, bold headings and subheadings for better search engine ranking.

Make Your Content More Accessible

Here are six more tips to provide your articles every opportunity for being read and enjoyed:

1. Use short paragraphs. When paragraphs are too long, the reader can easily lose interest and move on

to another article. You want to use white space and make it easy for the reader to skim your article. If she finds it interesting, she can then go back and read your article more thoroughly.

2. Make use of numbers or bullets. Numbers and bullets can quickly make the point accessible and easy to digest.

3. Use sub-headings to sub-divide your paragraphs on the page. Doing this makes the information more accessible to the reader and will increase the likelihood of your article, and resource box, being read.

4. Provide a good attention-grabbing title for your article. This will encourage readers who are interested in your topic to click on your article.

5. Keep your reader captivated from the title through to the end of the resource box. Share stories, tips, and solutions that will benefit your target audience.

6. Utilize statistics and facts, when applicable. Using statistics and specific facts can heighten the interest in your article because it becomes authoritative as well as specific.

Submitting Your Articles

Once you have your articles written, you need to submit them to one or more online article directory. There are literally scores of directories online, but not all are created equal. To achieve your aims of traffic generation and reputation enhancement, you want to submit articles to directories that are well-respected and actually used by online and offline publishers to find quality content.

Here are a few directories to explore:

EzineArticles: www.EzineArticles.com

Ezinearticles.com is a well-respected leader in the article marketing field. Creating your account is free and will take only minutes. The site includes lots of videos and help topics to get you going. You are limited to submitting ten articles until your article quality is confirmed. They also offer a paid, premium service that provides quicker publication, scheduled release of your articles, and more.

HubPages: www.HubPages.com

If you want to add video, photos, or other media types—beyond basic text—Hubpages.com may be for you. Create a hub and add content, driving traffic to your blog. A robust community and help section are there to assist you. HubPages offers free account creation and article submission.

LadyPens: www.LadyPens.com

If you are looking for a high-quality, "boutique," article directory, Ladypens.com is a great choice. You must apply to be selected as an author; once you are accepted, your chances of having your articles picked up by article publishers are very high.

Articlesbase: www.Articlesbase.com

Articlesbase is another popular, basic, article directory. You can create a free author account; and, once your articles are published, you can review extensive statistics regarding views and clicks.

Associated Content: www.AssociatedContent.com

A Yahoo!-affiliated content network, AssociatedContent.com includes over 2 million pieces of content (articles, videos, images). It is free to create an account, and you can actually earn money from advertising and revenue sharing.

In most cases, the first time you submit your articles, you are going to need to register with the article directory. If you intend to submit to a large number of article directories it is a good idea to set up a separate email account for this process so that you can easily store your article directory information in one, convenient location. This approach also allows you to keep any notifications or promotional emails sent out by the directories out of your main email inbox.

One thing to keep in mind is that many directories will allow you to submit the same article to multiple directories. Check each directory's specific guidelines and terms of service. Submission services such as SubmitMoreArticles (www.SubmitMoreArticles.com) allow you to upload your article once and then submit it to numerous sites, giving you bigger bang from your writing efforts.

When submitting articles to directories, it's not always quantity over quality. I would much rather zero in my efforts on a small number of high-quality directories than spend a lot of time submitting to hundreds of low-quality ones. Keep this in mind as you plan your article-marketing strategy.

Remember, the goal is to get targeted readers who are drawn into your article and motivated to click through to your website – and even better, to get them to republish your articles on their blogs and in their Ezines and newsletters. This will happen when you do your homework, choose great article directories, write quality articles and give a clear call to action, directing readers to your blog via a link in your resource box.

Repurposing Your Articles

Once you've gotten the hang of writing and submitting articles, you will see that it can become an easily integrated part of your daily or weekly writing routine. Once those articles are created and submitted to an online directory, don't stop there! Here are just a few ways that you can repurpose your already-written articles:

- **Create audios and videos.** People learn in multiple ways. Some prefer the written word; others prefer audio or video. Serve your audience by recording your articles as audios or videos. You can use the exact same content, just record in a different medium, and then post it to your blog. To further your reach, you can also add your videos to YouTube.com or other video-sharing sites.

- **Republish them on your blog.** While you may not want to publish the identical article on your blog, you can change it a bit. Rework the title and order, combine multiple articles together and add images to make your blog post different from your original article.

- **Create an eBook.** Once you have ten or twenty articles written, why not combine them together and create an eBook? Add an introduction and a conclusion, rework the text to make the transitions smooth, add graphics and formatting, and you have an eBook that you can give away or sell on your blog.

- **Develop a collection of guest blog posts.** Guest posting—where you submit a blog post on someone else's blog and link back to your own blog—is a fantastic way to get inbound links and to increase your exposure to new audiences. Take the articles you've written and slice and dice them so that you have a selection of posts available when guest-posting opportunities arise.

- **Make them into Tweets, status updates, and other quick posts on the social networks.** Take a longer article and break it into pieces which you can use on Facebook or via Twitter. Link back to your blog or to the original article, so people can click through for more information.

There are dozens of ways to re-use content once it is created. Make it a habit to find at least two additional ways to use any articles you write. You will soon find that you have more material—and more readers—than you know what to do with!

If there is one thing authors want more of, it's readers! Whether you are blogging for pet lovers, dentists, or baseball fans, driving more people to your blog is a prime objective. One of the best ways to drive traffic to your blog or website and to become known as an authority on your topic is through article marketing.

As mentioned, turning your article into a video is a great way to repurpose your content and attract more viewers and buyers. In the following chapter we will be focusing on video marketing and showing you how you can easily add video to your book marketing mix.

Keys to
Article Marketing Success

- Make a list of four or five topics you'd like to write about that would be of interest to your audience.

- Select one topic from this list and jot down three key points related to this topic. You now have the outline for your article. Compose a 400-500 word article on this topic.

- Take care to craft a catchy title and include keywords in your title as well as in your article.

- Carefully compose your resource box so that people will read it and take action by clicking on your link.

- Set up your account at EzineArticles.com and upload your article to their site. Be sure to add your photo and author information to your profile.

Article Marketing Resources

Articlesbase:	www.Articlesbase.com
Associated Content:	www.AssociatedContent.com
EzineArticles:	www.EzineArticles.com
Google:	www.Google.com
HubPages:	www.HubPages.com
Issuu:	www.Issuu.com
LadyPens:	www.LadyPens.com
YuDu.com:	www.Yudu.com

Chapter Seven:
Promote Your Book with Online Video

Video is the most effective way to connect with your audience because they can both see and hear you. This medium permits viewers to get to know you and find out more about your book. Web video is hugely popular on the Internet these days and it is expected to remain so for years to come. It is more powerful than audio yet simple to produce.

Adding video to your website and marketing campaign is one of the smartest things you can do. Video captivates your readers, provides them with a warm welcome and keeps them on your site longer, so they are much more likely to take action. *Having a video on your website or blog is essential.* It personalizes your approach, it creates interest in what you are offering, and people will be inclined to spend much more time on your site than they would have if you did not have the video.

If people like your video and if they find it moving, very informative, or even funny, they will send the link of that video to people they know, either through email or by posting the link on the social networks. This reaction to your video effort has the potential for a huge ripple effect!

Creating Web video might seem intimidating; the truth is that it can be easy, affordable, and even free. Creating Web video can also be a great deal of fun. You can either record your message with the camera facing you or you can create a screen capture video and record something that is displayed on your computer screen. The technology has advanced to the point where it is easy to record a video, even if you are not a technology expert.

How Authors Can Use Video to Market Their Books

Let's talk about some of the ways that authors can use video. You can have a webcam right on your computer monitor, click record, and begin speaking about various aspects of your book or your topic area. There are many things that you can do with these videos:

Create a video book trailer. Market your book by creating a video book trailer which you can post on YouTube and your site. You can create PowerPoint videos where you share your table of contents and spend a few minutes giving your viewers an overview or a guided tour of what your book covers. A video book trailer is a short video or multimedia presentation that helps to promote your book. Typically, it is less than two minutes, and a thirty-second to one-minute video can have even more impact, as people are more likely to watch it all the way through. The goal of your video trailer is to get people emotionally involved in your book by identifying a pain or a challenge and sharing a solution.

The simplest way to create a video trailer is through the use of images, PowerPoint slides, video clips, voiceover, music, and sound effects that paint a story that invites your viewers to get emotionally involved in your book.

You can also stand in front of your camera and tell the viewer about your book. This is not so much of a book trailer but rather a book interview or review. This type of video can also be considered more of a commercial than a compelling marketing piece. There is a time and place for this type of video, but let's not confuse this with a brief book trailer.

Read a chapter of your book aloud. You can either create a webcam video or a PowerPoint video of you reading your book. This is a wonderful way to connect with your audience as authors have been doing readings in person at bookstores for decades. You are simply keeping up with these technological times to reach a much larger audience of prospective buyers.

Record a video interview. Have someone else ask you a series of questions related to your book. Create a webcam video of you sharing an aspect of the book, why you wrote the book, and how people can benefit from the content in your book.

Create a video book. We've all heard of audio books. What about creating a video book? You can create an abbreviated, separate video for each chapter and take your reader on an audio-visual journey through your book. This also provides you with an upsell product and/or a special give-away for those who purchase your book during your book launch or through a special promotion. At the same time, it is a teaser opportunity to get them to buy and read the entire book.

Create a PowerPoint video. You can show the cover of your book, a picture of you, and several slides with bullet points and related images. Put the URL of your website at the bottom of each slide, record your voice, add some background music, and you have created a PowerPoint video that can be uploaded to YouTube.

Types of Video Technology

Webcam Video

One form of Web video is where you are sitting at your desk, you turn on your webcam or Flip camera and you begin speaking. There is a lot to be said for this format. It is fast, easy, affordable, and effective. Your viewers get to know you and learn to like and trust you. You can set-up a webcam right on top of your computer screen and this makes it really easy to get into the habit of recording a video at least once a week.

Before recording a video, you want to look behind you and see if the area is clear, clean, and attractive. You do not want it to be cluttered, which can be distracting. You want people looking at you and paying attention to what you are saying, so you may need to be a little creative with your backdrop. One option is to have a solid-colored wall behind you. Another option is to have an attractive oriental screen in back of you. A third option is to have a neatly arranged bookcase behind you.

Camcorder

I use the Logitech 9000 webcam and have it right above my computer screen. Logitech camcorders, like many other video cameras, have the microphone built in so you are all set when it comes to being able to record both audio and video. I recommend that you shoot your videos in 720p HD (high definition) for a high quality video. You can always decrease your video resolution but you cannot increase it. By recording in the wide format of HD, your video will look more current and professional.

Screen Capture Video

Another very popular type of Web video is called screen capture video. This is where you create videos from content that is on your computer screen. You can record a live Webinar, a PowerPoint presentation, a tour of a website or a software program, and much more. One of the easiest ways to create a professional screen capture video is by using PowerPoint. Create your presentation, then open up Jing Project (for videos under five minutes in length) or Camtasia Studio (for longer videos) and record your video as you go through the slideshow. Of course, you will want to record an audio narrative to accompany your presentation.

One easy way to turn your articles into videos is to use PowerPoint. This software program lets you create various slides; and, then, you can put those slides together into a slideshow, which can be exported to video. This technique can be simple if you already know PowerPoint, but there is a bit of a learning curve. Each slide in your presentation should represent a different paragraph of your article, and you can add special animations, effects, and photos to spice things up.

Video Software

Jing Project

Jing Project (www.JingProject.com) is a free screen-capture video program from TechSmith that allows you to record up to five minutes of video. This is actually an ideal amount of time to get your message across and it is easy to upload to YouTube. Jing Project videos make great tutorial videos for your learning library. No fancy equipment is necessary. This platform is perfect if you have a client who is asking a specific question. If displaying your computer screen will help in your explanation, then you can use this platform to do just that. Take a moment and download your free Jing Project software and make your first video today. You are going to love it and wonder how you ever lived without this tool!

Camtasia Studio

If you are thrilled with Jing Project and five minutes is not a long enough video for you, consider upgrading to Camtasia Studio (www.CamtasiaStudio.com)). There is a charge for this program, but they do have a thirty-day trial period. With Camtasia Studio, you can create videos of unlimited length and there is much you can do with the software. On the Camtasia Studio website, you will find dozens of tutorial videos that will walk you through every aspect of the program. Your PowerPoint program allows for integration between Camtasia Studio and PowerPoint so that you can easily create a video—with audio—of your PowerPoint presentation.

Windows Movie Maker for the PC and iMovie for the Mac

Another simple option is to use the video software that is installed on your computer. For example, if you are a PC user, you may already have Windows Movie Maker on your computer, while Mac users have access to a preinstalled copy of iMovie. You do not have to download anything. Just click on the webcam on your computer or your laptop, click on the record button, and share a message from your book.

Once you've created your videos, you will need a place to post them.

YouTube: the Number One Video-Sharing Site in the World

As mentioned in Chapter Three, YouTube is one of the most visited websites in the world and is considered, after Google, to be the second most accessed search engine. When people want to learn something, they can simply go to YouTube and look it up, the way many of us used to look for answers to our questions in an encyclopedia.

Uploading a Video to YouTube

When setting up your YouTube account, it is important to create one under the name by which you want to be known as this assists with branding. Therefore, if you are using your pen name or your real name, create your account under that name. If you want to be known for a specific topic, create an account with a login name related to that topic. For example, if you are known for teaching gardening tips, choose a login name such as "gardenmagic."

Go to YouTube.com and log in with your Google account. If you do not have a Google account or you want to have a separate Google account for YouTube, you can create one on that page. Also, it is very easy to upload a video to YouTube by following the step-by-step instructions.

To further brand your YouTube channel, you can select the colors and images that you would like to be displayed. This also creates an attractive environment for your viewers.

The disadvantage to posting YouTube hosted videos on your blog is that when people click on your video, they end up on YouTube! To avoid this situation, you can upload your video to a program such as Easy Video

Player (www.TryEasyVideoPlayer.com) and, then, people will not click off of your site when they click on your video.

If you do embed YouTube videos onto your site, it is important to properly select your settings so as *not* to include related videos in a playlist that shows up on your site. This action will prevent your viewers from being solicited away from your site as well as prevent you from inadvertently sharing questionable or suggestive video content.

YouTube Video Tips

* When you are posting videos on YouTube, they should be between three and five minutes in length even though the maximum length allowed by YouTube is fifteen minutes. By keeping them within the preferred three to five minute range, people are more likely to view your videos in their entirety. This characteristic will make it more likely for them to embed your videos on their websites, so that their viewers can enjoy them, thus providing you with exposure to new audiences.

* Since people are currently going to YouTube looking for specific subject matter, any video content you produce should be available there. One advantage of keeping your video content at YouTube is that it allows you to monitor how popular each of your videos are by seeing how many times they have been watched. To view your video statistics, visit the uploaded video section of your YouTube channel. You can access the "insight" tab next to each of your videos. This will provide you with statistics such as numbers of views, when people viewed your video and which country they viewed your video from.

- When you upload your video to YouTube, you have the opportunity to add keywords to the upload page. One mistake people make is that they do not maximize their opportunity to make it easier for interested viewers to find their content. When people go to Google to search for something, they rarely put in a single word. Instead, they type in several words. We call this a keyword phrase or a long-tail keyword phrase. For example, if you are posting a video about growing summer squash, your keyword phrases could be, "how to grow summer squash", "growing summer squash", and "planting summer squash," for example.

- Add value to your YouTube Station by creating a "favorites" section as well as a playlist of additional content that is going to be of interest to your viewers. In essence, YouTube is a social network, an encyclopedia, and a marketing site all rolled into one.

Having a YouTube channel is a great way to grow your reach and your followers. Here are a few easy strategies that you can put in place from day one: Once you have your YouTube station set up, your site design selected, and one video uploaded, you can begin to grow your viewers and your friends. An easy way to do this is to search for other channels on your given topic. View a few of their videos and, if you like their messages and approaches and believe that their content would be of value to your audience, add them as "friends" and subscribe to their channels. You will get viewers to your YouTube station, as people will see that you are linked to channels that they subscribe to and they will want to check out your videos as well.

Other Video Hosting and Video Sharing Options

UStream

To create a live broadcast television station, set up an account at UStream (www.UStreamTV.com). This is another free video site that you can brand with your colors and images or logo. You can either have a live TV show on any topic you'd like to share information on, or you can pre-record your show and upload the recording. Webcam video is very effective for an online TV show.

While your show is airing on UStream, you can elect to have a chat box available for your viewers. There are pros and cons to Ustream. For instance, in addition to your show, there is a lot going on at the site, and viewers can easily become distracted and click off of your site. However, a major plus to Ustream is that you can easily reach a wider audience.

Professional-Looking Videos on Animoto

Visit Animoto (www.Animoto.com), where you are able to upload images and video, select music, and add text. It is a snap to create Animoto videos that look highly professional. Furthermore, Animoto provides the option for you to upload your Animoto videos to YouTube. Once your Animoto videos have been uploaded to YouTube you will be able to share them with the world.

Interactivity with ooVoo Video Chat

ooVoo (www.oovoo.com) is a powerful business tool which offers an affordable solution for video conferencing, desktop sharing, and other communication capabilities—right from your personal computer. There are free as well as paid options, depending on your needs. With oovoo, your viewers do not need to download anything; they just click on the link to your video. The easier you make it for people to access your content—with the minimum amount of frustration, the more likely you are to connect with them and have the opportunity to build an ongoing relationship.

Spread the Word

Once you have a few videos, you will want to begin to create a buzz and share these videos with the public. You can begin by writing press releases announcing your new video and inviting people to view it. This is a great way to get new traffic to your website. You can also harness the power of the social networks by posting a video on Facebook. Invite people to visit your website to find out more about your book or to sign up to get three more tips on your topic, for example.

Be sure to post a video on your website, welcoming your visitors and inviting them to join your community (subscribe to your list) and receive weekly video tips, a video chapter of your book or a special report on your topic area. You can also display a video book chapter on your own website. This will create lots of attention and help to qualify your buyers, as they will be able to get a taste of the content of your book.

Keys to
Video Success

- Set up your YouTube channel with your branded username and colors. Add a profile image or logo.

- Create a PowerPoint or screen capture video using the free Jing Project software. Upload this video to your YouTube channel.

- Record a video of you speaking about your book and upload the video to your YouTube channel.

- Set up a free account at Animoto.com and create a thirty second video using photographs related to your topic. Upload this video to your YouTube channel.

- Send out a series of tweets on Twitter inviting people to view your videos.

Video Resources

Animoto:	www.TheBlogStation.com/animoto
Camtasia Studio:	www.CamtasiaStudio.com
Easy Video Player:	www.TryEasyVideoPlayer.com
Jing Project:	www.JingProject.com
ooVoo:	www.oovoo.com
Press75:	www.Press75.com
Learn Camtasia:	www.ScreencastVideoProfits.com
UStream:	www.UStreamTV.com
YouTube:	www.YouTube.com

Unlock the Secrets

My hopes are, that having gone through the content in this book, you have a clearer idea of how you—as an author—can harness the power of the Internet to grow your brand and your reach, and to sell more books.

I've come up with a fun acronym to help you remember the topics discussed in *Book Marketing Made Easy*. That acronym is the word "VIBRANT". Each letter in the word represents an essential facet of your online marketing campaign. The word "vibrant" also evokes excitement, high energy, and vitality—all worthy attributes to emulate. You will find that there is a chapter dedicated to each of these key, marketing activities.

V = Video Marketing

I = Information Marketing

B = Blogging

R = Relationship Marketing

A = Article Marketing

N = Networking

T = Teleseminars

Let's review!

V is for Video Marketing

An essential facet of online book marketing is video marketing. Video is the most effective way to connect with your audience, as they can both see and hear you. Video allows them to get to know you and it is an amazing tool for building trust and relationships. Web video is the hottest thing on the Internet right now and it will be for many years to come. It is more powerful than audio and easier to create now more than ever before.

There are several options for creating Web video. You can use a camcorder or your computer's webcam to create a "talking head" type of video where your viewers see you on the screen. Another type of video is known as screen capture video. This method allows you to easily create video tutorials, PowerPoint videos, video book trailers, and more. You simply select a portion of your computer screen to be shown and verbally share your message with your viewing audience.

I is for Information Marketing

Information marketing is taking the content of your book and turning it into a wide variety of products. You can create an audio book, a video book, an eCourse, a coaching program, or an online course, to name just a few. Information products are fantastic for increasing profits, credibility, traffic, and book sales.

By making your content available to people in a wide variety of formats, you will not only increase your bottom line, you will also create a community of loyal fans who will want to know what other products and programs you offer. By developing your relationship with your readers, they will not only notice what you are doing, they will help promote you and your work.

B is for Blogging

Your blog is not just where people go for content. Your blog is where they go to connect with you, thus blogging is another essential facet of online book marketing. Your blog can be the hub of your online empire. This is where you build community and credibility. It is where you share the message of your book in writing as well as via audio and video. A blog can also house a special area for members as well as your online store.

One of the biggest benefits of blogging is that Google and other search engines love blogs; the frequently updated content, the links to and from your blog, and the repeat visits result in higher search engine rankings. Blogs are interactive, which distinguishes them from other websites. Therefore, your blog can help you to build relationships with your customers, prospects, and website visitors through two-way communication. People will be able to quickly and easily share their comments and suggestions with you, which will help you better understand them and respond to their needs.

R is for Relationship Marketing

Relationship marketing is all about marketing second and building relationships first. After all, people want to do business with people they know, like, and trust. Relationship marketing produces fans who not only rave about you but refer you to other people without your even asking. It is about building a strong community of people, who come to see you as a go-to person because they know that you care about them and they know that you are knowledgeable.

Relationship marketing is the key to growing your business. By building positive bonds with people, they will want to know you, to refer others to you, and they and their associates will want to do business with you. In order for people to get to know, like, and trust you, you need to find effective ways to connect with them, bring value to them, and begin to build a relationship with them. There are a variety of ways that you can build relationships, trust and credibility with your audience. First and foremost, you must become known as a "giver"—someone who cares about others.

A is for Article Marketing

One of the best ways to drive traffic to your blog or website and to become known as an authority on your topic is through article marketing. You will gain exposure to new audiences and have more opportunities to share your message and sell your book. Posting your articles on an article directory offers a very important benefit; blog owners and newsletter publishers can use articles from article directories in order to provide more content for their readers. As long as they leave your resource box and live links intact, they are permitted to publish your articles. Think of the leveraged opportunities available to you by using article marketing.

N is for Networking

Online networking is much like networking offline. You need to find effective ways to connect with people and bring value to them and thus begin to build a relationship with them. Social networking is a powerful way to grow your network, your brand recognition and your business.

Social networking, just like in-person networking, is about building relationships— not selling your products or services to people. Instead, sell them on *you* and create raving fans. You can brand your online image by having professional-looking profiles on the social networking sites. Join in the conversations on Facebook, share information and ideas on Twitter, provide informative and entertaining videos on YouTube, participate in LinkedIn groups, feature your book on the social networks for authors, as there is much opportunity for interaction and idea sharing.

T is for Teleseminars

One of the most powerful ways to build relationships with people is via Teleseminars. Teleseminars provide a way for people to hear your voice and feel your enthusiasm. They get a sense of who you are. As an author, providing ways for your audience to connect with you and hear the message of your book will increase your book sales and your reach. Teleseminars easily provide you with a platform to connect with your audience.

Teleseminars also provide you with the raw material to create additional books as well as a wide variety of additional products and programs. From audio recordings, which can be sold as downloads or CDs, to an eCourse or eBook created from the audio transcripts, the possibilities are seemingly endless.

Now It is Time to Take Action

Whether you use one or all of these VIBRANT marketing strategies to market your book online and gain exposure as an expert in your field, you have before you a roadmap for growing your following and increasing your book sales.

To begin with, choose one of these strategies. Apply what you have learned in this book and get comfortable with the techniques. You will find that each of these strategies is easy to grasp and that they will have a powerful impact on your online presence and your book sales.

My gift to you, to assist you in this process is a **free** *Quickstart Guide to Book Marketing.* You can find out how to access your copy by flipping to the back of this book.

Here's to your book marketing success!

Dvorah Lansky

Acknowledgements

Connie Ragen Green and Dr. Jeanette Cates, thank you for inviting me to participate in your online revenue workshop. The time that we spent brainstorming and identifying my niche focus and then developing an online course that would benefit professionals in that niche, nonfiction authors wanting to learn how to market their books online, has expanded my business, brought more joy and prosperity into my life, and formed the foundation for this book. You are both exceptional educators and anyone who has the opportunity to learn with you is indeed fortunate.

Donna Kozik, thank you for developing your "Book in a Weekend" course. Your positive and joyful attitude and knowledge of book writing and book publishing, made participating in your course both delightful and worthwhile. What took me seven months to accomplish with my first book, you pulled out of me in a weekend. Here's to celebrating your goal of helping one thousand authors publish their books in a weekend.

Bob Jenkins, thank you for being an incredible mentor and guide on my success journey. Your exceptional clarity and ability to help me to refine my ideas, marketing materials and programs, has allowed me to accelerate my goals, products, income and success.

Lynne Klippel, thank you for sharing your heart-centered approach to book marketing. By applying the lessons you taught in your course I have been able to approach my business from a deeper place within myself, thus, my joy for what I do and the success which I am experiencing has grown exponentially.

Alfred Poor, my amazing publisher, thank you for your council, wisdom, vision, and for believing in me.

Kathleen Gage, thank you for helping me take my business, my brand, and my income to the next level. Your positive attitude and high standard of excellence inspire and motivate me.

To the incredible book marketing experts who participate as speakers in my *Book Marketing Teleseminar Series* and as contributing authors for the *Book Marketing Gazette*:

> Sue Collier, Lucinda Cross, Judy Cullins, Kristen Eckstein, Tony Eldridge, Kathleen Gage, Bob Jenkins, Connie Ragen Green, Daniel Hall, Shelley Hitz, Shel Horowitz, Brian Jud, Lynne Klippel, Donna Kozik, John Kremer, Reno Lovison, Jill Lublin, Roger C. Parker, Joanna Penn, Caterina Rando, Dana Lynne Smith, Steve Taubman, Michelle Vandepas, Val Waldeck, Beth Kallman Werner, Jennifer Wilkov, Terry Whalin and Lisa Robbin Young.

Thank you for your friendship and for sharing your wisdom, expertise and programs with our members and students.

About the Author

D'vorah Lansky, M.Ed.
Author and Marketing Wizard

D'vorah grew up in California where she received her teaching degree. She went on to Cambridge, Massachusetts, where she earned her M.Ed. in Creative Arts in Education. D'vorah has travelled the world. As an educator, one of her most rewarding experiences was working as a volunteer with Ethiopian elders and youth in Israel. D'vorah taught in traditional classrooms for close to two decades. When her son was born, she began her career on the Internet. She has been marketing online and mentoring entrepreneurs and business professionals to grow their businesses since 1994, using offline and online marketing strategies.

D'vorah is the author of *Connect, Communicate, and Profit: Build Successful Business Relationships Online,* is the publisher of the *Book Marketing Gazette* and the producer of the *Book Marketing Teleseminar Series.* Her work has been published in *Chicken Soup for the Network Marketer's Soul, Corporate Mom Dropouts,* and *Ignite Your Passion.*

D'vorah coaches and trains authors in online book marketing practices. She is passionate about online marketing as well as helping authors grow their business and their brand.

D'vorah's premiere training program is an online course called, "How to Market Your Nonfiction Book", where she provides a step-by-step approach to developing an effective online marketing campaign.

Connect with D'vorah

I love hearing from new and seasoned authors and invite you to connect with me at:

- www.Twitter.com/marketingwizard
- www.Facebook.com/AuthorsMarketingCircle
- www.LinkedIn.com/in/themarketingwizard
- www.BookMarketingTeleseminars.com
- www.BookMarketingGazette.com
- www.HowToMarketYourNonfictionBook.com
- www.AuthorsMarketingCircle.com

Here's to your book marketing success!

D'vorah Lansky

Also by D'vorah Lansky...

Connect, Communicate, and Profit:
Build Successful Business Relationships Online

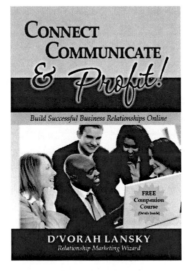

In *Connect, Communicate, and Profit*, D'vorah Lansky presents you with the strategies and techniques that you need to get up to speed quickly on the basics of Internet marketing. Learn how you can easily create a bridge between your online and offline networking and business-building practices.

In today's busy world where things move quickly and technology is king, you must have a vibrant and interactive online presence. When you apply certain basic principles of relationship marketing, you will grow your network, build awareness of your brand, and position yourself as an expert in your field.

Connect, Communicate, and Profit is designed for small business professionals and entrepreneurs who want to market online, or who know that they need to be marketing online but are not sure where to begin.

What Others Say about
Connect, Communicate, and Profit

"Forget the arduous process of trial and error that your competition is relying on. D'vorah has done all the research for you, and gives you the prioritized steps and cost-effective resources right here in this book."

Bob Jenkins, author of *Take Action, Revise Later*

"Let me make this simple. If you want to build a huge network of people who think about you, care about you, trust you and most importantly, refer you...but you only have a few minutes a day to do it, then you need to buy this book **today** and devour it. What more can I say?"

David Frey, CEO, Marketing Best Practices

"The content provides a valuable survey of Internet marketing methods, offering a wealth of information and recommended resources. The material is very practical so you can start using it right away. The depth of content also offers plenty of room to grow, so that you continue to benefit from it as you evolve your skills."

Joan Pagano, author of *Strength Training for Women*

"The next best thing to hiring D'vorah Lansky as your relationship marketing wizard is to read her book and apply her expertise to your business. Be prepared for explosive growth!"

Marge and Bruce Brown, Quantum Results Coaching

Get your copy today at:
www.ConnectCommunicateProfit.com

Get Your <u>FREE</u> Quick Start Guide To Book Marketing

Take Your Book Marketing to the Next Level Now!

<u>Includes a Customizable Book Marketing Checklist</u>

Now that you've read *Book Marketing Made Easy* and have access to **the keys to success** at the end of each chapter, it is time to put your book marketing knowledge into high gear!

- Are you worried that you won't follow through and get the results you deserve and desire?
- Would you like to have a handy reference on your desk to know exactly what to do and when?
- Would you like to have access to the best book marketing resources for authors?

I created this quick start guide to help you put the keys to success into action so that your book sells like crazy and you become a highly sought after author and speaker.

As you now know, whether you self-published your book or went through a traditional publishing house, the work of marketing your book falls primarily on your shoulders. This guide is designed to make that process easy and accessible to you.

Enjoy a concise and easy to follow action guide so you can apply what you've learned in this book.

The *Quick Start Guide to Book Marketing* will provide you with an easy to follow, printable reference to keep you on track, towards your book marketing goals. Get ready to:

- Streamline your book blog for maximum impact
- Leverage the best social networks for authors
- Host and appear on teleseminars
- Access the best online resources for authors
- Track your marketing activities and results

In addition to this handy guide, you will have access to our "Book Marketing Made Easy" and "Authors Marketing Circle" community of motivated authors.

Start today by downloading and printing out your *free* copy of the *Quick Start Guide to Book Marketing* and put the keys to success into action!

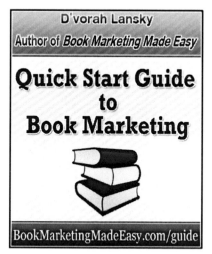

Print out your <u>free</u> copy of the
Quick Start Guide to Book Marketing now at
www.BookMarketingMadeEasy.com/guide